# THE UNTOLD VOYAGE

BY THE SAME AUTHOR:

*Voyages of a Simple Sailor*
*Mingming & the Art of Minimal Ocean Sailing*
*Mingming & the Tonic of Wildness*
*Mingming II & the Islands of the Ice*
*Mingming II & the Impossible Voyage*
*Travels Through a Window*

TRANSLATIONS:

*Rogue Waves by Michel Olagnon (Adlard Coles)*
*The Adventures of Laforest-Dombourg Volumes 1 & 2 by Eric*
*Gautier*

ROGER D. TAYLOR

# THE UNTOLD VOYAGE

*F*

*THE FITZROY PRESS*

Cover illustration: Roger D Taylor
Published by The FitzRoy Press 2025

𝓕
**The FitzRoy Press**
9 Regent Gate
Waltham Cross
Herts EN8 7AF

The manufacturer's authorised representative in the EU for product safety is Authorised Rep Compliance Ltd, 71 Lower Baggot Street, Dublin D02 P593 Ireland (www.arccompliance.com)

ISBN Print version: 978 1739214 265
e-book: 978 1739214 272

A catalogue record for this book is available from the British Library

Publishing management by Troubador Publishing Ltd, Leicestershire, UK

*For Lárochka, wherever you may be…*

*'Tis all a Chequer-board of Nights and Days*
*Where Destiny with Men for Pieces plays:*
*Hither and thither moves, and mates, and slays,*
*And one by one back in the Closet lays.*

*Stanza XLVIX from The Rubá'iyát of Omar Khayám,*
*translated by Edward Fitzgerald*

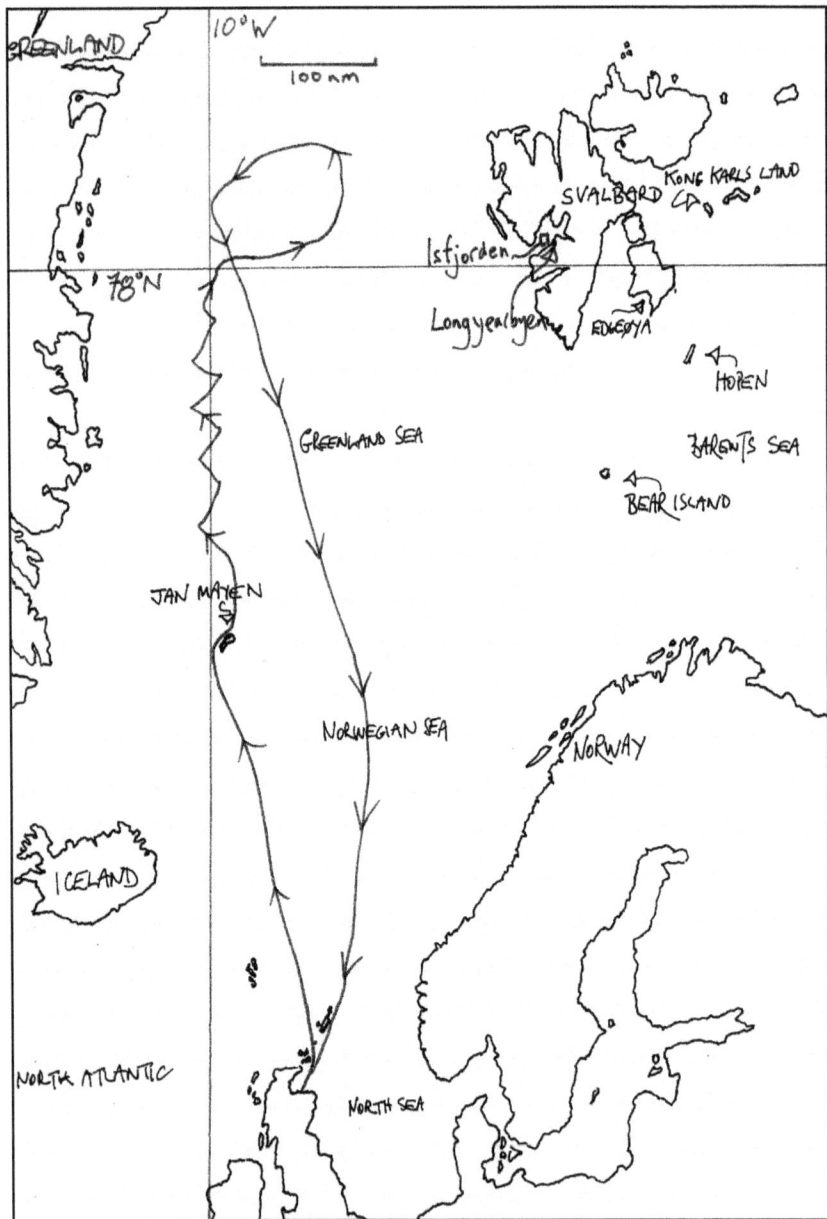

GREENLAND

10°W

100 nm

78°N

SVALBARD

KONG KARLS LAND

Isfjorden

Long year byen

EDGEOYA

HOPEN

GREENLAND SEA

BARENTS SEA

BEAR ISLAND

JAN MAYEN

NORWEGIAN SEA

NORWAY

ICELAND

NORTH ATLANTIC

NORTH SEA

*The approximate track of the untold voyage.*

# 1

There are some tales that are best left untold. This is perhaps one of them, but I shall tell it anyway. I am an old man and it is an old man's tale and so I have little, if anything, to lose by its telling. It is a tale, too, of the sea, and therefore it must be told, as the sea will always have the last word.

*

For many years I had been sailing my little boats to the distant wastes of the Arctic. Every summer I had made a long voyage to some unimaginable corner of the Far North. To sail away, alone, for months at a time, far from land, far from what we are pleased to call civilisation, had become a deep-seated need, a compulsion. It was only in those wild, remote places that I could find true communion with myself.

I had written many books about these voyages, telling things just as they were, and as best I could. I had tried to tease out the poetry of solitude; to fathom the beauty of every passing wave; to feel, if only for the briefest of moments, complicity with the living things for whom that alien world is home.

My voyages had, in the main, passed without drama or incident. Long experience had taught me how to prepare and manage my craft with the minimum of fuss. The principles of simplicity and patience had served me well for many thousands of miles of voyaging. Crossing the oceans, year after year, in my tiny cell, I had become a kind of solitary monk: contemplative, peaceful, at ease with myself and the world.

＊

There was, however, one voyage… and what happened on that voyage was so far beyond the compass of what I thought possible that I have never, until this moment, said or written a single word about it. I ask myself why this should be and can find no answer. Fear? Shame? Guilt? I do not know. Perhaps all of them; perhaps none. The human mind is a complex, contradictory creation. Despite my years, I lay no claim to any understanding of the workings of my own psyche. As an observer and writer, I have trained myself to look and see and tell. If I can discern any purpose to my existence, it is that: to look and see and tell. For once, I had failed. I had looked, I had seen, but I had not told.

Well, the time has come. Every excuse has been stripped away. I must now find the strength and the will to set sail once again and recount what happened during that fateful summer.

2

The voyage began like any other: the long drive with my yacht *M.*, as I shall call her, in tow. I had made this journey many times, always to the same little fishing harbour on the ironbound coast of the Moray Firth. It was the ideal departure point for a voyage to the Arctic. With a fair wind it was possible to be north of the Shetland Islands within two or three days, away from land and oil rigs, fishing boats and commercial shipping lanes. My aim was always to reach a spot at least two hundred miles from shore, in a depth of at least two thousand metres, as quickly as possible. Only then could I relax.

As usual, I arrived at the harbour late in the evening. I parked alongside the quay and even at that hour was welcomed by old friends from the village. These were hard men, born to the sea, staunch as the low granite cottages that wound their way up from the inner basin. They had grown accustomed to my form of Sassenach madness. They no longer shook their heads at the sight of my little cockleshell, less than twenty-one feet in length. They no longer asked how I could possibly put to sea without an engine. They no longer suggested that the voyages I had in mind were little short of madness. I had made enough departures from their haven and, more importantly, enough returns, for them to accept that I knew my business. Over time, I had earned their grudging acceptance.

*

By midday the next day *M.* had been craned into the harbour and her mast dropped into place. Rocking gently at the pontoon that would be her home until we set sail, she had once more taken on an almost living persona. The next few days were spent setting up her sail and rigging, moving all my stores aboard and stowing everything below in as shipshape a fashion as was possible in such a small yacht. As was my usual habit, I had enough food and water to last me for a hundred days of nonstop voyaging. I expected to be at sea for about sixty to seventy days, and so had plenty of margin for survival, should something unforeseen extend the voyage beyond its planned duration.

*

Every year, I planned a new route around the High Arctic. The basic idea was to penetrate as far north as was feasible into seas that were rarely, if ever, sailed. The reduction in sea ice over the last five or six decades now made previously unthinkable trajectories possible. I had already sailed to what even recently would have been considered absurdly high latitudes: 79°, 80° and even 81° North. Each voyage has its own target, its own roughly pre-planned shape. This time, my aim was to see how far north I could reach in the area off the north-east coast of Greenland. If the ice conditions allowed, I might even be able to penetrate close enough to catch a glimpse of the land. On the way there, I hoped once more to skirt past my favourite island – Jan Mayen. To sail well to the north and west of that magical and little known protuberance was a challenging prospect, as the Arctic ice makes its way south down the Greenland coast. In this remote north-west corner of the Greenland Sea, on the very fringes of the Arctic Ocean, the water is truly cold, unlike the warmer waters of the Gulf Stream which flow north up the coast of Europe.

Some years previously, I had sailed off the central coast of eastern Greenland, in the relatively modest latitude of 72° North. Sixty miles to the east of Scoresby Sound, a great indent in the Greenland coast, I had encountered sea ice and been forced to withdraw. Since then, my trajectories had mainly been to the west and east of Spitsbergen and as far north and east as Franz Josef Land, well to the north of the Russian mainland.

The annual reduction in sea ice is by no means linear, and so each spring and early summer I kept a close eye on the extent and movement of the ice. This enabled me to decide what would route might be feasible and when would be the optimum time to set sail.

I will not go into too much detail on all of this. This book is more about the singular incident that overshadowed and defined that voyage, rather than about the technicalities of high-latitude sailing, about which I have already written at great length. I hope, then, that the sailors amongst my readers will forgive me for passing quickly over the finer and more arcane intricacies of sea-going that they love so much.

# 3

As I worked away preparing *M.* for sea, my mind began its disengagement from the land. This is a long process that begins on shore and lasts some weeks into each voyage. A man cannot achieve harmony with the wild places if his head is all a-jumble with the usual press of everyday thoughts. The whales and dolphins and fulmars and the very waves of the ocean itself have no concern for bank balances or the currency of a bus pass. To have even the faintest chance of grasping some understanding of what that other life is, or perhaps might be, a man's mind must be free of every worldly concern. He must empty himself of all that he is and become an open, unflinching receptacle for a new world of impressions.

Lying in my bunk each night, caressed by the lapping of the water against *M.*'s hull, breathing slowly and deeply, I began the transformation from a social, land-based organism, suffused with all the usual pettiness, into something other. What that 'other' might be is almost possible to define. It is a kind of blank canvas, ready for whatever may be painted on it, or drawn, or scratched, or inscribed, or rubbed, or hammered. For me, it is the absolute prerequisite for looking, seeing and telling.

*

I had the usual run of visitors. Some were old friends from thereabouts, come to say hello, others were casual onlookers, curious about *M.'s* unusual appearance and rig. I showed the newcomers how *M.'s* Chinese sail worked, demonstrating the ease with which I could raise or lower it, the latter done in a couple of seconds using just one hand. I gave my usual quick lecture on the mechanics of the self-steering gear, that marvel of engineering which allowed me to spend months at sea without touching the tiller.

The more inquisitive were permitted to have a look down her single watertight hatchway to the cabin below. With my water and stores now aboard and well-stowed, there was little space down there: a single berth to starboard, an alcohol stove to port with a movable chart table over it. The forward berths had been reduced in length by the watertight bulkhead I had installed and were given over to stowage; the port quarter berth – a narrow bunk set further aft beneath the cockpit - was similarly taken up with all the stores and spares needed for a long voyage.

There were the usual comments about how unthinkable it was to spend so much time on the high seas in such a small space. I nodded as graciously as I could. Time and space are relative: after a week or two at sea, or even less, my cell always transforms itself into a veritable palace.

*

One afternoon, when I was lying on my bunk after my usual frugal lunch, enjoying the calm of the day and the growing anticipation of my imminent departure, I was woken from my meditation by a gentle knock on the side of the hull. I pulled myself off my berth and stuck my head through the open hatch.

On the pontoon was a man I had never seen before. Bronzed, silver-haired, white-bearded, lean of face and with limpid blue eyes, everything about him signalled a man of the sea. With his faded cap, well-worn blue jacket and deck shoes, here was the very incarnation of a seadog, an old salt, a shellback, a sea rover, a jack-tar.

He lowered himself to a crouch so that his face was level with mine. He looked at me closely for a second or two, his piercing blue eyes locked into mine. There was something disconcerting about his calm, unhurried gaze.

*Roger?* he asked. His voice was soft, with a Scottish inflection.

*Yes.*

*Ye'll nae know me.* There was a pause. *I'm Joshua.*

His eyes roamed around *M.'s* deck and rig.

*That's a fine wee boat ye've got there.*

*Thankyou. Are you local?*

*Local?* He smiled, showing a row of even white teeth. *Och no. That's fifty years now I've been in Australia, the Pacific, you know? I'm juss back hame for a wee while and that's me off again.*

*I spent many years down that way myself.*

*Aye, I know that. That's why I wanted a wee word.*

*Do you sail?* I knew it was a redundant question, but it came out anyway.

*Aye. A wee cutter. Sirius. As bonnie a boat as ye'll ever see. Timber. Twin companionways. Built by Wrights of Brisbane. That's nearly thirty years I've sailed her. Nowhere in the western Pacific I've nae been.*

I was trying to guess his age. 75? 80? Perhaps even more. He was still crouched down, lithe and comfortable.

*Would you like to come aboard?*

*Och no. She's your ship an' I'll leave her to you. I juss wanted a wee look. It's the Arctic you'll be headed to?*

*Yes.*

*Nae the first time, so I've heard?*

*No. Maybe fifth or sixth. I'm losing count.*

*Well, I admire what ye're doin'. That cold is nae for me.*

His eyes fixed mine with a burning intensity. Their translucent blue seemed to glow.

*You take care. The sea, now, ye ken. You never can tell.*

He held out his hand and I leaned over to grasp it.

*Thanks, Joshua. Thanks for coming down.*

He fixed me with a final stare.

*Dinnae forget. Ye take care. Ye take care.*

He stood up and walked off along the pontoon. As he reached the top of the ramp up to the quayside, he turned and raised his arm high in a final farewell. Within a few moments he was gone.

# 4

I had been hoping to set sail sometime in the last week of June, subject to a run of favourable winds. There had been years when persistent north-easterlies had kept me trapped in port, but this year I was lucky. As I was finishing my preparations the wind settled in from the west-south-west, with a forecast for more of the same for the coming days. On the morning of the twenty-fifth of June, my old friend the harbourmaster towed us out of the awkward entrance to the harbour with his little workboat. Once we were a short distance offshore, I raised the sail and cast off the tow.

Here I must make one more technical digression which I hope will be the last. My Chinese junk sail is made up of six horizontal panels, with the joint between each panel supported by a carbon-fibre batten. Think of a sail that opens or closes somewhat like a fan, or a window blind. With such a sail I could therefore carry anything from one panel, for very strong winds, up to the full six panels, for extremely light winds. This gave me the flexibility to be able always to carry exactly the right amount of sail for the conditions. All the halyards and control lines were led aft to the hatch. I could stand in the hatch, with just the upper part of my body exposed to the elements, and do everything necessary for controlling the rig without having to go out on deck.

The same went for the self-steering system attached to *M.'s* stern. Once again, all the control lines were led to within easy reach of the hatch. I could change course, or our angle of sailing to the wind, standing on the steps of the companionway, the short ladder that led below.

All this meant that I very rarely had to exit the hatch to go on deck. I could manage the yacht for days, or sometimes weeks at a time, without leaving the warmth, dryness and relative safety of the cabin.

There is a common misconception that the singlehanded sailor spends his time glued to the tiller, out in the elements from dawn to dusk or even longer. This is no longer the case. It can sometimes happen when things go wrong. I had to spend many weeks steering on deck when crossing the Tasman Sea from New Zealand to Australia many years ago, after my self-steering system was destroyed in a storm. For long Arctic voyages, my habitat was my relatively warm little cabin, not the exposed deck.

Another misconception is that life in this little cabin must somehow be claustrophobic. Not a bit of it. Over the hatch is a folding canvas hood, somewhat like a pram hood, that allows me to keep the hatch open, or partially open, in all but the worst of conditions. In fine weather I can sit on the top of the companionway steps, head and shoulders out of the hatch, and with the canvas hood folded down, observe the whole watery world in perfect comfort.

*

With a fair wind from the west-south-west, *M.* needed no more than four panels set to drive her comfortably north, or more accurately, slightly east of north. I set the self-steering, coiled and stowed the towline and settled in to my usual position in the hatchway. The harbourmaster made a few last-minute circles around us, taking photographs as he went, and with a final wave sped off landwards.

We were on our own and heading once more for the Far North. I sat in the hatchway, heart swelling at the thought of the adventure to come. Occasionally I looked astern to watch the Moray hills dip lower to the horizon. A guillemot flew across our now foaming wake. Far ahead on our port bow, a blue and white fishing boat mooched around in the unpredictable way that working fishing boats always mooch. A weak sun broke through the clouds to our west and with the wind freshening we raced further and further offshore, I reduced the sail to three panels. *M.* surged forward with a will and there we were once more: man and boat in perfect unison, heading joyfully towards whatever lay beyond that ever-receding horizon.

## 5

The wind forecast turned out to be incorrect. That did not surprise me in the least. Every sea area covered by the Shipping Forecast is vast, and the brief synopsis for each one can only ever be a rough generalisation. I had long since learned to sail for the weather I had, rather than the weather that may or may not arrive. This helped to keep me locked into the present moment, undisturbed by false fears or unfounded hopes.

On the evening of the twenty-seventh of June, when we were two and a half days out from harbour, the wind backed to the south before falling away completely. I lowered the sail and lashed it tightly to the tubular stainless steel frame that hinges up from the cabin top. We were twenty or so nautical miles to the east of the Orkneys, and so were able to drift north or south, without any concern, pushed by the weak tide, rolling gently on a calming sea. I slept on and off, setting my alarm to wake me up every fifty minutes so that I could check the horizon for ships or fishing boats. At this time of year, at that latitude, night scarcely falls. I saw occasional ships' lights well to the north, heading east and west through the Fair Isle passage.

*

At six in the morning I ate my breakfast, the remaining third of the previous night's dinner, heated in my sole nine-inch saucepan. I have a rule never to sleep between breakfast and lunch, however tired I might be, as too much sleep leads to lethargy.

I sat in the hatchway, watching the inevitable entourage of fulmars paddling around *M.,* and listening to their raucous squabbling. For the moment we were going nowhere, but this did not bother me. To the south-east the sun was already high in a sky marred only by the thinnest haze.

For the first time since setting sail, I thought about my strange visitor – Joshua.

He had caught me at a moment when my mind was elsewhere, and I now realised that I had missed the opportunity to find out more about him. He said he had spent fifty years in Australia and the western Pacific. He seemed to know me. Maybe he had read my books. Somehow, I sensed that there was more to it than that. I tried to reconstruct our brief conversation. The more I thought about it, the more annoyed I was that I had not insisted that he come on board, that I had not asked him more about himself. Why had he made the effort to come and visit *M.*? Where had he come from in

Scotland? I had assumed he had just walked down from the village, but was that really the case?

I thought again about his slightly knowing smile and another thought struck me. Had we met somewhere before? I too had been in that part of world, fifty years ago. I too had once owned a yacht called *Sirius* when in Australia, but she was a 21-foot open keelboat that I had sailed on the Swan River in Perth. There was no connection there. I too had sailed the Queensland coast. Had our paths crossed? I have a good memory for faces, but would I remember a face after half a century? What would he have looked like as a young man? I searched my memory but could find nothing.

And what about his final words? They now rang in my ears like a warning: *ye take care, ye take care.* Were the words no more than casual politeness, or was there a deeper sense to them? The more I thought about it, the less I understood.

The surface of the sea began to darken on the eastern horizon and before long patches of catspaws idled past, ruffling *M.'s* ensign hanging lifeless from the top section of the lowered mainsheet. Within half an hour a light but sailable breeze had filled in from the east. I raised the full sail and settled *M.* to our new course: due north. If this wind held, we would pass to the west of Fair Isle via the southern passage, and continue straight on, leaving the island of Foula and the whole of the Shetland Isles to our east.

Yes, we would continue straight on. On and on: seven hundred nautical miles or so dead ahead lay our next objective – the island of Jan Mayen.

6

The first few days of any voyage are always easy to recall, but as the days merge into weeks the many threads of the daily detail become harder to unravel in retrospect. That is why I am always fastidious in the keeping of my two ship's logbooks. Alongside the official ship's log, in which I note down all the minutiae of weather, navigation, sail changes and so on, I keep what I call my personal log. This is a less formal notebook in which I write down any random thoughts, ideas and impressions, however offbeat or seemingly irrelevant they may be. Used in tandem, these two logbooks enable me to reconstruct a voyage with, I hope, an appropriate balance between the factual and the imaginative.

I make this point because it is now the time to make the first of several confessions. It pains me to make this admission, not least because it flies in the face of all the sea-going conventions to which I have adhered for well over half a century. Moreover, not only is it a breach of the rules of good seamanship, it is also, in a word, shameful. I am not a religious man in the conventional sense, but throughout the years since I made that voyage, my inner ear has, on an almost daily basis, been tormented by that most succinct of liturgical phrases: *Forgive me, Lord, for I have sinned.*

The simple fact is that, well before the end of the voyage, I tore both my logbooks to shreds and threw their remnants overboard. The reasons for this grotesque act may become clearer as my story progresses, but no amount of rationalisation after the event can expunge the self-disgust I now feel and always will feel. It was, I freely admit, an act of cowardice. It has taken me some considerable time to find the courage to redress the balance as best I can, by relating what happened during that summer, but it is, I fear, much too little and much too late.

# 7

With the unmistakable hump of Unst, the most northerly of the Shetland isles, now low on the eastern horizon, and with the breeze now freshening from the east-north-east, bringing us a little harder onto the wind, we left the last of the land astern and plunged blissfully on into a wide open sea. As ever, my spirits soared. We were now unchained, liberated, free to roam unhindered wherever winds and fancy may lead.

*

From here on we would be on our own. I carried only two methods of communication: a mobile telephone, for which there was no signal once a few miles offshore, and a hand-held VHF radio with a range of just a few miles. To be thus cut off from all long-distance communication and to cross the seas untracked has always been central to my concept of adventure. In this age of satellites, it is an increasingly outmoded approach. Technology invites compromise and I have always preferred to remain resolutely uncompromising. Ultimately a man must shift for himself, whether for better or for worse.

For several days the wind held in the east, sometimes backing a little, sometimes veering, but always allowing us to hold our direct course for Jan Mayen. With the North Atlantic Current helping us along, our daily runs held steady at eighty to ninety nautical miles. I could not have asked for a better start to the voyage.

*

We sped on north, bucking and plunging through a beneficent sea, settling to our task with an easy will. Straight-winged fulmars traced their endless patterns over the waves. From time to time an arctic skua or two hung high over the masthead. Just once, the fin of a male orca, tall, erect, electrifyingly purposeful, cut past us at a terrifying speed.

We were once more subsumed into a world I knew so well, a world that I could love and hate in equal measure. The pages of my logbooks began to fill as I dissected everything I saw and felt. That was, after all, my task. Those logbooks are gone, consigned to the depths of the Greenland Sea, and time and a need to forget have erased most of their content from my memory. The scribblings of my personal log, in particular, are beyond recall. No doubt there was the usual mix: descriptive phrases quickly jotted down to capture the essence of a moment; unbridled ramblings of a mind now set free from its land-based constraints; obtuse mathematical analyses of fanciful concepts; comic interludes. It is as well for a sailor not to become too grandiose, and I had learned to keep my own pretensions well in check by means of a constant mockery of all the alter egos I carried with me as crew: the idle Cabin Boy, the prissy Collector of Rain, the surly and implacable Distributor of Nuts, the Ship's Doctor *and* Dentist.

All I can remember is that I was in as good a form as I had ever been at that early stage of a voyage. I knew well enough that were we to get close to our target in the north-west corner of the Greenland Sea, there would likely be dangers and difficulties to cope with, and that I would have to exercise the greatest caution, especially as regards sea-ice. The prospect of danger in no way dulled my optimism. I have always been an instinctively defensive sailor, wary of the heroic gesture and ready to make a graceful retreat in the face of threat.

The sea is the greatest of levellers. As each day passed, bringing us closer to the first major nexus of the voyage – the Arctic Circle – my sense of confidence, and my belief in the *rightness* of what I was doing, grew stronger. I was not so stupid as to feel invincible, but I had become, I suspect, sufficiently relaxed and complacent to think that the sea, in all its many moods and intricacies, could no longer surprise me.

# 8

As far as I can recall, it was late on the eighth day of our voyage that we crossed the Arctic Circle and so entered once again that unworldly realm of constant daylight. For several days the wind had been blowing steadily from the south-west, bringing with it the low cloud and murk that characterises these latitudes in mid-summer. Warm air blowing over a cooler sea condenses to the fog in which we now found ourselves. Visibility was often down to just a few hundred yards; from time to time the mist lifted enough to give a brief glimpse of an indistinct horizon. I had sailed this route many times and well knew the smothering, suffocating claustrophobia that these endless days of fog can induce. They are to be endured rather than enjoyed, but they are the necessary rite of passage that leads to an eventual liberation, if one is lucky, beneath the crystalline and coppery skies of that most wonderful of meteorological phenomena: the Arctic High.

*

The sea was not yet empty of traffic. A series of receding foghorn blasts somewhere to the west suggested a ship heading south; perhaps a cruise liner. One day I could hear the hum of engines for several hours: probably one of the pelagic fishing vessels that one often meets hereabouts. There was always the possibility of meeting another vessel until we were clear of Jan Mayen, and so there was no let-up in the rigour of my watchkeeping.

I can no longer be sure of exactly what I thought about, sitting hour after hour in *M.'s* hatchway, watching the curl of a million passing waves. It is easy to fall into a kind of trance, what with the regular rise and fall and roll of *M.'s* easy motion, and the soothing sound of the water rushing past under her lee. Life stands still and simultaneously rushes forward. All is movement and all is stasis. My mind is a fixed centre around which all the phenomena of the world race and revolve; my body falls through time and space. At sea, these seeming contradictions can start to resolve themselves, for there, the purification of the mind, leading to an inner stillness, is somehow stimulated by the incessant motion of the waves. Here are two poles of the same unity, each one necessary to the other.

*

The wind held and the fog persisted. From time to time we emerged into a clear patch, transforming the sea from grey to deep indigo under the brilliance of an un-swaddled sun.

This was a promise of what may lie ahead, but it never lasted: within a few minutes yet another horizon-wide bank of murk had overwhelmed us.

At noon every day I pencilled a cross on my chart showing our position, calculated how far we had sailed since the previous day's cross, and entered all the details in the ship's log. This ritual, the centrepiece of the navigator's art for many centuries, set the basic rhythm for each day. Once completed, it was time for lunch: bread and cheese, a home-baked flapjack and half a Granny Smith apple. Lunch was usually followed by a short nap and an afternoon in the hatchway watching the world. Many solo sailors load up with books for a voyage and spend hours lying on their bunks reading. The only books I carried aboard *M.* were for reference: navigational tables, almanacs, identification books for seabirds and whales. To be able to spend several months on end wandering the wildest of places is a privilege and I have always wanted to be present in every waking moment of every day. To take oneself out of the here and now by immersing oneself in a book seems to. be a negation of the adventure itself. Every second is precious. There is always, always, something to see, something to learn, something to contemplate. To spend hours reading is to switch off from the actual, to turn one's back on the limitless nuances of the sea and the sky and the creatures that inhabit them. I want to extract and distil the essence of every detail, for it is only in the patient, painstaking accretion of minutiae that one has any chance of finding a way into the heart of wildness.

*

It was my habit to prepare my evening meal at about 6pm – a panful of packaged rice or pasta mixed with tinned vegetables and fish. A third of this was retained for breakfast. Dessert was rice pudding, or flavoured custard, or bottled fruit, followed by a slice of home-baked fruit cake. Over the years I had honed my cooking so that all my meals could be prepared quickly and easily, using the minimum of fuel for my single burner stove.

During the twelve hour gap between dinner and breakfast I ate either nothing, or very little. If conditions meant that I was very active during this period, changing the amount of sail set, managing the self-steering system, or maintaining long periods of watch at the hatchway, I would eat an energy bar or a few handfuls of homemade trail mix.

It was a simple and efficient system of victualling, especially as the components for the main meals were all packed into large waterproof containers, each one clearly labelled with its contents. This way, I never ate more, or less, than planned, and always knew exactly how many days' worth of stores remained.

*

Four or five days after the crossing of the Arctic Circle, the wind fell away, leaving us to ghost gently forward under the full mainsail. A more persistent sun burned away at the engulfing mist until there, at last, was the full circle of the horizon: north, south, east and west. We had emerged once more into an open and infinite universe. The shadows cast by the mast and sail on the side decks crisped and darkened, and the sea burst into a light show of a million dancing reflections and blinding scintillations. For the first time on this voyage, I heard the gentle exhalation of a minke whale keeping tabs on us somewhere off the port beam. I sat in the hatchway until late in the evening, feeling blessed beyond measure, happy in my work, as confident as I could be that nothing could mar the harmony of the voyage. Towards nine in the evening, I cocooned myself in my sleeping bag and slept, waking every hour or so to check a horizon still razor sharp under the eternal sun. The minke whale stuck with us, and so throughout the night his occasional *pffff* provided a reassuring counterpoint to the regular rise and fall of my own respiration.

# 9

*Alone, alone, all all alone, alone on a wide, wide sea.* I had now reached that state of grace incomprehensible to the landsman; a state beyond solitude, beyond the mundane, beyond the strictly temporal; a state now free of the oppressiveness of the quotidian. Yes, there were still hours in the day, there were still matters of navigation and ship management to attend to, but these were now mere adjuncts to the greater and more noble task of the surrender of the self. The wide, wide sea invites that surrender, though it is not easily given. To entrust oneself to the enormity of the sky and the ocean and the distant stars requires a certain mix of bravery and carelessness, a knowing stupidity, the nature, perhaps, of a Holy Fool.

In any event, I was now at complete ease as we drifted softly on, subsumed unconditionally into the whatever, the whenever, the however. I could now give myself over to a glorious solipsism too, for there was now nothing but me, the lone sailor, along with the infinite sea and sky. All had been stripped away bar my relationship with that sea and that sky.

*I sail, therefore I am.*

I sat in the hatchway in the morning sunshine and realised why, for a whole lifetime, I had found this sea-going so edifying, so necessary. It was the ultimate *reductio ad absurdum*. There was no better way to lay bare one's body and soul. Every long voyage was a shriving of the inner self, a stripping to the bone, followed by a rebirth and a rebuilding. With each reconstruction, I became a little stronger, a little more resilient; I knew myself, my strengths, flaws and weaknesses, a little more intimately. At sea, all alone, there is no place for dissembling or obfuscation or trickery. Every failing and dishonesty will be exposed. The sea, as cold and merciless as it is seductive, leaves no place to hide.

# 10

Despite our much reduced rate of progress in the failing breeze, we were now only a day or two's sailing from the southern tip of Jan Mayen. My mind was ranging ahead to thoughts of that wondrous creation: from south to north a mountain ridge, a low saddle and then a stupendous volcanic cone, almost seven and a half thousand feet high, the whole mass pushed up in near verticality from the depths of the Norwegian Sea.

I had sailed the coast of Jan Mayen three times previously: twice northbound up the east coast and once southbound down the west coast. It was my intention, if conditions allowed, to pass for a second time up the western side of the island, firstly to maintain some equilibrium in my visits, but more importantly because I wanted to give myself up, for a second time, to the unmitigated exhilaration of sailing close in beneath the towering cliffs that lead eventually to the summit of the volcano, Mount Beerenberg. Cutting down through these cliffs are the vestiges of two once-mighty glaciers, the Kjerulf and the Weyprecht. I dearly wanted a second, and probably last sight of them. Before long they will be gone; before long I too will be gone. I felt a strong need to say farewell.

*

My memory of the next day or two is vague. I remember that there was a pod of northern bottlenose whales ranging around what was now a placid sea. They worked their way here and there, from horizon to horizon, with no discernible pattern, a group of perhaps four or five of them. Their position and presence were signalled from time to time by a flurry of breaths as they surfaced as a group and rolled clumsily forwards.

The sea temperature was falling noticeably, making the cabin colder, and I think it was around this time that I put on warmer clothing – woollen thermal underwear, thick socks now worn under moonboots, track suit top and bottoms and a heavy woollen sweater. When below I wore a faux-fur Russian-style shapka; if working outside in the hatchway I always changed my headgear to a waterproof baseball-style hat with ear coverings. I had sewn a makeshift chin strap onto this hat, to make sure that it could not blow off in even the strongest winds.

There was of course no way for me to wash and dry clothes on these voyages, so I took a large store of clothes packed away inside waterproof bags. These bags were labelled and stowed aft in the deep recess above the port quarter berth. I used a boathook to pull them out when needed. Used clothes went back inside the same bags.

My main memory, before the contours of Jan Mayen started to push up over the northern horizon, was a feeling of profound contentment. There are times like that at sea, when it seems that nothing can trump the deliciousness of solitude and a tiny self-built boat advancing sweetly across an infinite sea and sky. Thought drifts off, to be replaced by the raw sensation of aliveness. There is nothing but the moment, the undercurrent of a beating heart and a sense of almost total integration into the surrounding scene. I was capable of spending many hours sitting in the hatchway, head empty of thought, in a quasi-meditative state, tingling from top to toe with the wonder and strangeness of it all: one tiny sphere amongst a trillion, trillion others, spread across unimaginable distance and time, and I, a strange and provisional organism, somehow endowed with life and a few basic powers of perception, making my way across a deep and restless fluid somehow covering most of this sphere, blown by currents of air somehow generated by the interplay of heat and cold and relative pressure; the whole lot in essence no more than the playing out of physics and the mechanics of matter (whatever that may be); and yet, to my eyes anyway, so ineffably beautiful.

*

I seem to recall that I was awakened from this dreamy state by a starkly mundane interjection: the top sections of the mainsail and jib of a yacht making its way north-west were just visible above the north-eastern horizon. Such wind as we had was still light and patchy, and the yacht's steady progress suggested that it might be motor-sailing. I could not pick up the sound of an engine, but the yacht was a fair distance away, and downwind too.

Using my binoculars, I watched the sails for a while. I was no longer all alone on a wide, wide sea. This was a disappointment, but the sight of another sail is always galvanising for the lone sailor. The questions pile up. Where is the yacht from? Where bound? How many aboard? What kind of boat? Something about the profile and configuration of the sails suggested that it was a fairly small craft. Maybe it was another solo sailor, bound too for Jan Mayen. Maybe our paths might cross. I considered unpacking my little VHF radio from its waterproof case and trying to contact the other vessel. Given that it was hull down over a distant horizon, I suspected that even if whoever was aboard was keeping some sort of radio watch, my signal might not reach. In any event, I did not try, preferring to continue my quiet and solitary meandering unannounced. I did not much welcome the enervation of unexpected human contact. Having found my ideal sea-going equilibrium, I had no wish to upset it.

Before long the sail disappeared below the horizon. I tried to reestablish my previous mood, but it was no good. It was hard to return to thoughts of the universal and the eternal with so many petty and unanswerable questions about the yacht I had just seen buzzing around inside my head. It would soon be time to eat, anyway. I ducked down into the cabin and started to prepare my evening meal.

# 11

The wind veered slightly to the west and began to strengthen a little. I snugged the rig down to four panels of sail and set a course to take us to a point five miles or so to the west of the Sørkapp, the south cape of Jan Mayen. The island lies on a south-west to north-east axis, so from there I would change course to the north-east and run up the west coast. If this breeze held it would be ideal, angling slightly into the coast but allowing the possibility of moving quickly offshore again if need be.

The wind shift brought another benefit, clearing away a bank of cloud to our north and unveiling the lofty shoulders of Mount Beerenberg. Some high cloud was still wound around the summit itself, but the central portion of the mountain, still streaked with patches of snow and ice, hung like a magnet above the northern horizon.

For many years this peak had taunted me. On my first two visits to Jan Mayen, it had been completely shrouded in cloud, leaving me disappointed and only able to guess its shape and height. On my third run past the island, I had fared better: brief holes in the cloud streaking past the summit had allowed for several momentary sightings of the rim of the crowning volcano. For the first time I could piece together the contours of the mountain from sea to summit.

The problem with Mount Beerenberg is one of basic meteorology. Warmer air coming in off the Norwegian Sea is forced upwards towards the top of the mountain, cooling and condensing as it goes, and forming clouds. For the peak to stand out in complete clarity, unblemished, requires specific weather conditions. Maybe this time I would be lucky.

*

I can no longer recall, or even work out retrospectively, the exact date when we made our landfall just to the west of the Sørkapp. The further I advance with this story, the more indistinct all the elements of time become. This is not helped, too, by the fact that we were now in twenty-four hour daylight, and so no longer had any divisions of night and day to help isolate and pinpoint certain events. Everything took place under the unending and somewhat strange light thrown by a sun tracing its low parabolas over the horizons.

As we neared the southern cape, I started to make out the unusual conical hills which push up close inland. I had seen similar landforms elsewhere in the Arctic, on the islands of Kong Karls Land, to the east of Spitsbergen, for example.

These hills form almost perfect cones and are so regular and symmetrical in shape that they seem not to belong to the more chaotic landscape from which they have erupted.

It was of course midsummer, and all of the land had taken on a luminous green sheen from an explosion of plant life, no doubt mainly mosses and lichens, which now clothed every available surface. The cliffs and hills and ridges rising from the sea seemed to glow, and as ever when making a landfall after an extended passage, I was bewitched by the richness of the textures and colours and infinite detailing of the land.

I lowered a panel of the sail and set a new course to the north-east. With the wind on our port quarter, we could run easily up the coast, skirting past the Hoybergodden, a broad square headland just north of the southern tip of the island. Jan Mayen is about thirty miles in length and so with a fair wind we could be clear of the north cape within half a day.

*

Were I writing about any other voyage, I would doubtless by now have introduced some element of humour into the narrative. The whole idea of an old man setting off alone into the Arctic, as if he were some latter day Nansen or Jackson or Peary, is ripe with absurdity. That absurdity has always been apparent to me, and I have been quick to puncture any hint of overblown affectation with the needle of self-mockery. By laughing at myself, and by winkling out the many ridiculous elements of the enterprise, any potential pretensions are kept in check. As my old nemesis, the Ship's Distributor of Nuts, may have put it: *You ain't Scott of the*

*Antarctic, sunshine, just a stupid old bugger with a head full of nonsense.*

For this story, however, I find it impossible to add even the slightest comic touch, that last sentence aside. As will become evident as the tale unfolds, to make light of this voyage, or any aspect of it, would be grossly inappropriate. I am writing at this point about our progress north, progress which unfolded sweetly, almost joyfully, but every word I write, every recollection I drag up from my reluctant memory, is tainted and weighed down by the knowledge of what is to come. I hope, then, that I will be forgiven the untypically sober tone of my writing. In this instance, I have no choice in the matter.

# 12

We settled in for our run up the west coast of Jan Mayen, and for the next few hours my heart sang. The sky was slowly clearing of cloud, save for one or two of the majestic cigar-shaped masses that can develop hereabouts. Luckily, they were well to our east, away from Mount Beerenberg itself, and so for the first time I had an unimpeded view of the whole volcano. As was my habit, I busied myself taking photographs and videos of the mountainous ridge immediately to starboard and of the growing Colossus itself, still far ahead on the starboard bow. Before the end of the voyage, I deleted every single image and video file, determined as I was at the time to erase all records of those fateful weeks, in whatever form, and so I must once again rely purely on my visual memory to recreate a picture of that glorious day.

Jan Mayen has always exceeded my expectations. On every

visit I have uncovered more aspects of its charm and power. Each time I sail the island's coast, the spell it has over me grows stronger. It is difficult to explain this attraction. Perhaps it partly lies in the variety and harmony of the island's physical form, partly in the unlikeliness of its great peak surrounded by nothing but deep, deep ocean, partly in its remoteness and, until recently, its inaccessibility. There are all these physical aspects, yes, but there is something more that I find almost impossible to pin down and verbalise. The island satisfies an indefinable yearning. There is something immeasurably beautiful and sad in its timelessness. It evokes wonder and despair in equal measure. It is a reminder of both the age of the world and of the brevity of our passage through it. When sailing close to Jan Mayen, I feel bigger, stronger, somehow enhanced by the solidity of its mass, but at the same time I am overwhelmed by a sharper sense of my own insignificance and my own mortality.

This visit was no different. In fact, with Mount Beerenberg now dominating the north-east horizon, a towering mass of brilliant white, I sensed all the usual conflicting reactions with an even greater acuteness. It was almost unbearable to witness the strange and inexplicable beauty of this wild place and to feel myself more, and less, growing and diminishing, at one and the same time.

*

The low central isthmus that divides the narrow southern ridge from the huge circular base of Mount Beerenberg creates a shallow scallop on both the east and west sides of the island. I had set a course that would bring us in close to the north-west shoulder of the volcano, and so for a while we edged away from the land as we crossed this indent in the coastline. Now astern were some of the features I knew so well from my previous southwards run down this coast, in particular the Kvalrossen headland with its rounded offshore rocks. I assumed that Kvalrossen is a version of the Norwegian *hvalrossen* – walruses (the English word being derived from the Norwegian) but had no idea whether the headland was so called because of the whaleback shape of the outlying rocks, or whether the beautiful little bay to the south of the headland was once home to these magnificent creatures.

As the land started to rise into the foothills of the volcano, I could see once again the rock formation, on the top of a line of cliffs, which had so puzzled me last time. From the north one has the impression of a perfectly sculpted cube, so regular in shape that it looks man-made. This illusion does not hold so well from the south and I remembered with amusement that for a few minutes the outcrop had fooled me completely.

In any event, my eye was now drawn to the great mass ahead, devoid of cloud and illuminated by what must have been an afternoon sun. Here was a Mount Fuji, or a Mount Taranaki, thrusting straight out of the depths. From ocean floor to summit the mountain rises about fourteen thousand feet. The icy peak, with the rim of its volcano defined by a central flat section, was impressive enough, but what has always overawed me are the monstrous shoulders of the mountain rising almost vertically from the sea. We were now approaching these shoulders. With the wind still holding steadily from the west, I gave myself permission to sail in as close as I possibly dared.

*

The air above our wake was now alive with the criss-crossing flightpaths of hundreds and hundreds of fulmars. The sea too was spread with scores of bobbing birds. These fulmars had the mucky grey plumage of the northern variety, rather than the pure white heads and underparts of their southern cousins. The birds stuck with us hour after hour, as they always do, their wildness and inscrutability and incessant motion a counterpoint to the dark, immobile cliffs looming ever more deliciously overhead. We were angling gently in towards this great wall of rock.

As a precaution, should I need to change course quickly, I now disconnected the self-steering gear and took over the steering myself, using tiller lines that led to the hatchway. With *M.* under my direct control, I would have a better feel for how she was behaving and sense any change in the prevailing conditions much more rapidly. By sailing in so close to such a potentially hostile shoreline, I was taking the kind of risk that I usually avoided. It went against all my basic principles of good seamanship, especially as it was in one sense completely unnecessary. Yes, strictly speaking, or at least from a purely navigational point of view, it was unnecessary, but I was nonetheless compelled to do it. This compulsion arose from another need: to come face to face, literally and uncompromisingly, with the very essence of bleakness. To sail right in under that wall of rock, at the very ends of the earth, would terrify, exhilarate and refresh my aging spirit. It had to be done. It was possibly, I thought at the time, a final rite of passage, a last glorious reassertion of my own wayward nature.

I eased *M.* off the wind a few degrees more so we were now heading straight for the western extremity of the cliffs ahead. The base of Mount Beerenberg describes a gentle curve. Further around the curvature ahead lay the glaciers, cutting down from the summit in a north-westerly direction.

At this point we were probably still a mile or so offshore, but this distance was now reducing rapidly. One mile may seem, to a landsman, a considerable margin, but after several weeks of sailing the open ocean, to be so close to such an impossibly tall and implacable monolith, with the waves breaking on its base now visible, was more than disconcerting. I had to fight to overcome my natural aversion to sailing without good cause into a potentially dangerous position. Like the fool that I am, I carried on, not simply throwing caution to the wind, but risking everything in the process.

I admit that at that point I felt pleased with myself. For once I had overcome my inbred defensiveness and was about to do something bold, heroic, exceptional. I was thinking about the photographs and videos I would be able to take as we skirted the cliffs just a few yards offshore. My mind was already composing exquisite little phrases that would capture the wonder and drama of the moment.

We kept on in. I could now hear the surf breaking on the unforgiving rock at the base of the cliffs. My fear had almost gone, subsumed into the madcap deliciousness of the moment. The wind still held, and the fulmars still wheeled around us in their thousands, dumb witnesses to the unfolding spectacle. I may even have wished for a more appreciative crowd of onlookers; eyes more cognisant of what a brave chap I was, what an intrepid navigator.

We kept on in, and in short order two unrelated events changed the complexion of the day. There was a metallic bang aft, and the mainsail swung right out to leeward, spilling its wind and leaving us rolling helplessly. As I checked aft and aloft, trying to work out what had happened, I saw that my little masthead wind indicator was gyrating uncertainly. The wind was changing.

*Bloody hell!*

One of the blocks for the mainsheet, the long and complex line that controls the angle of the mainsail, had failed. It had parted company with its attachment and was now high up in the air. Its departure had allowed the mainsheet to run right out. This had happened to me once before, on the way to the Azores, also at an unpropitious moment. To repair the problem would take some time. I would have to lower the mainsail, dig out a new block from my stores, attach it aft and re-reeve the mainsheet. If I were lucky, I could do this in fifteen minutes, but with each swell carrying us closer to the cliffs, that may not be enough time.

*Bloody hell!*

I thought about the problem for a few more seconds and decided on a different provisional solution. I hauled in the mainsheet. As I expected, it was now no longer controlling the two upper battens of the mainsail, so the top of the sail was falling away to leeward, providing little, if any, drive. To counteract this, I eased the mainsheet and the mast parrels - the lines which control the set of the sail at its forward end - and hauled up the mainsail so that all six panels were set, then sheeted it in hard. It was an ugly sail, with a huge twist in its now liberated upper section, but the lower panels were still under the control of the mainsheet and would, I hoped, provide us with enough power to sail clear of the shore. Once safely away from the land I could make the full repair.

Had the wind held, it would have been relatively easy to edge away from the cliffs under this makeshift rig, but I was now paying the price for sailing in so close. Despite it being an onshore wind, the proximity of the huge rockface was setting the flow of the air all awry.

*

Yes, I had got myself into not just an almighty mess, but a perilous one, too. The wind died. Short-lived gusts came in from any old direction, backwinding the mainsail and leaving us gyrating helplessly on the shore-bound swell. I considered manning the oars, to see if I could keep us off the rocks by rowing, but I knew from a previous episode in an Icelandic fjord that I would not achieve anything except total physical exhaustion. In full cruising trim, still with most of her stores aboard, it was impossible to move *M.* in a seaway.

For the best part of an hour, I worked at the tiller and the mainsheet, trying to keep us in some sort of sailing configuration, to capture and retain some drive seawards, or at the very least parallel with the coast. From time to time little puffs of wind came in from a beneficial direction, giving us a few yards of positive movement, but in the main there was nothing but a useless, maddeningly gutless series of rotating eddies. We were well and truly stuck.

There was no question that we were being carried closer into the cliff-face, but watching the curve of the land ahead, I realised that we were also moving to the north-east, more or less parallel with the coast. I had no idea whether this movement was caused by tide, or current, or both; nor did I care. All I knew was that this flow of water might well save us from an ignominious and, in this instance, well-deserved fate. The land ahead angled more sharply to the east-north-east. There was at least a chance that the current would propel us on in the direction we were now moving, away from the breakers I could now hear pounding on the shore.

In fact, it was the wind that saved us. As abruptly as it had dropped away, the breeze suddenly resumed normal service, nice and fresh and still from the west. Within a few seconds we were careering forwards under our misshapen rig, carrying too much sail despite its inefficiency. Never mind that. The water was now creaming joyfully under our lee as I hardened up to a beam reach that had us heading at one and the same time in those two most desirable of directions: due north and away from land.

As we sped off, the first of the mighty glaciers, the Weyprecht, appeared to our east. I had previously sailed in close to this glacier and had intended, this time, to push in right to the very limit. Well, I had once again learned my lesson, and was now nothing but deliriously happy to see it falling rapidly away on our starboard quarter. I was done with the bold and the heroic.

*

Relieved and chastened, I hand-steered until we were well offshore, then lowered the mainsail and fitted a new mainsheet block. Astern, Mount Beerenberg, as brilliantly white and lofty as I had ever seen it, still dominated the skyline. I realised that there was something of the siren about this mountain. I had been drawn in to its beauty, seduced by its promise. I had become the gullible sailorman, too quick to yield, too weak to resist.

As we settled in once more to our northern trajectory, with the rig now snugged down and the self-steering gear back in operation, I resolved that for the rest of this voyage I would favour my usual caution, that I would aim for tranquility, calm, equanimity. There would of course be some risk-taking heading into the cold north-western corner of the Greenland Sea, but I would work hard to minimise any threats to our safe passage. I felt confident that I had the knowledge and experience to cope with whatever the ocean might throw at us. I see now that this confidence was no more than a continuation of my well-proven foolishness. On the other hand, no amount of reflection could have prepared me for what lay ahead. Some things lie beyond the powers of even the most fertile imagination.

# 13

My plan at this stage was very simple: I would sail due north, keeping as close as I could to the line of longitude 10° West, until we reached latitude 78° North. There, I would reassess the situation and decide how to proceed. I had chosen these coordinates because I was fairly sure, having studied the sea-ice maps for a while before setting sail, that we would not encounter ice on the way there. The sea-ice had already withdrawn to the west and to the north. There was a very good chance that by the time we reached 78° North 10° West, a straight-line distance of just over four hundred nautical miles, the ice would have receded much further, thereby allowing us to continue on north, and hopefully to the west too.

To sail due north along this line of longitude had two severe drawbacks. Firstly, the sea temperature would be falling rapidly. My little yacht's insulation, of which I will talk more later, would be put to a severe test. Perhaps more critically, we would be sailing directly into the south-going East Greenland Current. From a strictly navigational point of view, a better way to sail to the north-west corner of the Greenland Sea would be to keep well to the east, in the warmer waters of the north-going North Atlantic Current – the final part of the Gulf Stream – and follow the currents round, in an anti-clockwise direction, reaching the intended spot with a favourable current all the way.

There were several reasons why I had chosen not to take this easier option. Firstly, I had previously sailed twice from Jan Mayen to Spitsbergen, and had no wish to repeat that route. Secondly, I knew that in sailing directly north from Jan Mayen, I would be sailing in waters rarely, if ever, crossed by solo sailors in very small yachts. This was, as ever, a delicious prospect. The final reason was more prosaic: some hundred and twenty nautical miles north of Jan Mayen lies the Vesteris Seamount. This is a kind of submarine Mount Beerenberg: a volcanic peak, still active, whose summit lies just a few hundred feet below the ocean surface. I had for many years wanted to sail over the top of this volcano. I was particularly interested to see the effect that it had on the wildlife thereabouts. There was a good chance that the shallow water would attract fish, which would in turn bring in dolphins and whales, which would in their turn attract the seabirds that followed their pods, living off scraps. Would the air and water around the seamount be teeming with life? I wanted to find out.

*

As far as I can recall, the west wind held for another day or so, enabling us to strike out due north at a good pace. The peak of Mount Beerenberg descended slowly to the horizon until it was no more than a low and indistinct white mound. This final sight of the mountain reminded me of the sail I had seen some days previously. Where was that yacht now? Had it perhaps anchored on the east side of Jan Mayen, out of the prevailing westerly wind, so that its crew could go ashore? Perhaps to make an ascent of Mount Beerenberg? There is a small Norwegian scientific base on the island, and the mountain is regularly climbed. Or had the yacht sailed straight on to the north-west without stopping at Jan Mayen? I did not know, and I had no way of knowing. Moreover, the yacht was clearly faster than *M.,* so there was little chance that I would see it again.

I was still annoyed with myself for having taken such a stupid risk under the Mount Beerenberg cliffs. In retrospect, I was finding it hard to believe that I had been so cavalier, especially as I had plenty of experience of the tricks the wind can play close to high land. In this instance I had once again been lucky to be able to extricate us from a potentially disastrous situation, but it could easily have turned out differently. It was a while since I had thought about my visitor at the pontoon, Joshua, but I now felt those piercing blue eyes boring into me. I heard his words of warning: *Ye take care! Ye take care!* I had not taken care – far from it, and my annoyance with myself turned to shame. I had ignored the words of a kind old sailor who, it seemed, had made a deliberate effort to come to see me. Worse, I not really thought about them. I had heard his words but dismissed them as just another platitude. I really had to do better.

# 14

So far on this voyage the winds had been benign and favourable. We had had an unusually good run which was unlikely to continue much longer. Sure enough, not long after Mount Beerenberg had dipped below the southern horizon, the wind went round to the north and stayed there for what in retrospect seems like an eternity. It was not an especially strong breeze, mainly about a Force 4 on the Beaufort Scale, occasionally gusting up to a Force 5, but its air was cold and heavy, blowing as it was off the icepack somewhere to the north. Nor was it a wind that held stolidly in exactly the same direction. It was constantly veering and backing, within a sector from north-north-west to north-north-east. This had it advantages and disadvantages. Although it was impossible for me to sail the course I really wanted – due north – these variations enabled me to get a little closer to my ideal track.

The constant shifting of the wind meant that I was forever at the hatch readjusting the self-steering gear, tacking to find a more favourable slant, playing with the trim of the mainsail and the self-steering windvane to keep us moving well in the shortish sea into which we were ploughing.

It was hard work, twenty-four hours a day, with minimal reward, for as well as a headwind, we had a half knot of current setting us back. We were sailing well, but never in the right direction. Sixty miles of sailing through the water might, if we were lucky, advance us twenty miles towards our objective. Well, I had been in that situation often enough, and there was nothing for it but to buckle down, day after day, and watch the daily crosses on the chart move north at their own desultory pace.

I was not in the least downcast by this change of fortune, as my worry had been that we were advancing to the north too quickly. Every extra day and every extra week spent on the outward part of the voyage gave the ice more time to recede. The icepack usually reaches its minimum area in October, by which time the days are too short and the weather too bad. I had to find the sweet spot in which there was less ice, but still twenty-four hour daylight and relatively benign weather: neither too early nor too late. This long and difficult period of headwinds was potentially working in our favour by putting a brake on our progress towards the ice.

Even though we were advancing north only slowly, there was a palpable change in the feel of the sea and the sky. Above, a solid layer of cloud, just a few thousand feet high, poured down from the northern horizon, blocking whatever remaining warmth the sun may have provided. Below, the sea temperature was falling rapidly. The hull, decks and cabin top of my little ship are well insulated with thick foam which itself is lined with carpet. This takes the edge off the worst of the cold and stops any condensation forming. Nonetheless, I now had to wear thick gloves even in the cabin, and had pulled on a pair of snow-boarding trousers over my track suit bottoms. My knees started to ache – a sure sign that we were now truly into the Arctic.

\*

Despite the erratic, zig-zag course that we were now sailing in the constantly shifting headwind, I managed to pass within a mile or so of the crater of the Vesteris Seamount. I would have preferred to sail directly over the top, but given the conditions, this was as much as I could have hoped for. I spent more time than usual in the hatchway, well wrapped up and eyes peeled for any wildlife, but saw nothing out of the ordinary, just the usual mix of little auks, kittiwakes and Arctic terns that always frequent these waters in summer. There was no sign of whales or dolphins. Nor was there any hint of sea-ice, not a single floe or lump, which was reassuring.

On we sailed, day after day. Nothing much changed. The cloud kept coming, the sea stayed grey and cold, my knees ached. When the wind shifted to north-north-west, we sailed on port tack, and when it shifted back to north-north-east, we changed to starboard tack. When the wind came in from due north, not favouring either tack, I usually chose to sail on port tack, as it meant my bunk was on the more comfortable leeward side of the boat.

On we sailed, day after day, for more than two weeks, every day a repetition of the same rituals, every day bringing us just a smidgeon closer to 78° North 10° West. I still have my Arctic charts, but they no longer have any trace of this voyage on them, all my pencil markings having been carefully erased. Despite that, I remember well enough the pitiful trail of crosses snaking north from Jan Mayen.

I was not in the least despondent at this slow progress, despite its many frustrations. It is rare to execute a long voyage around the Arctic without at least one period of prolonged headwinds. I was well used to this kind of dogged accumulation of distance in the desired direction. In any case, speed has never been of much interest to me; the priority is simply to spend time at sea, as easily and as harmoniously as possible. I suspect that I even took a perverse pleasure in squeezing out our miserly northerly progress from an adverse wind and an adverse current. The contrary conditions were a fitting challenge to my innate stubbornness.

## 15

The narrative brings us now to 78° North 10° West, or thereabouts anyway. I think we crossed 78° North a few miles to the east of the target longitude. It is hard to imagine a more desolate, forgotten corner of the ocean. We were now some three hundred nautical miles to the west of Spitsbergen and its main inlet, the Isfjorden. The north-east coast of Greenland lay a hundred miles or so to our west. It had taken the best part of a month to get here.

At the time I was elated, and not a little pleased with myself, at having reached such an outlandish spot. As ever, the voyage was changing my conception of the planet. To sail to the remote places is to revise one's personal view of the world, to redefine one's relationship with north, south, east and west. One is not the same person here as one is there. One begins to apprehend the Earth's scale and strangeness, to learn that there are many worlds, infinite possibilities, layer upon layer, few of them knowable, most of them quite alien.

Yes, my mind and spirit were fizzing with the sweetness of the moment: 78° North, and perhaps more to come. With care, and not a little luck, we might be able to push on directly to 79° North, or even 80° North.

*

How foolish I was; how blind. I was about to get my comeuppance, but in such an inconceivable manner that even now I still shudder at its brutality. I started to write the story of this untold voyage as a kind of expiation, but I am now having doubts about whether I can continue with the tale. Thus far it has been an unthreatening task, with the heart of the matter still some way off. But now only a few miles of grey and frigid sea separate us from the moment when…when what? I struggle to find the right phrase. The words coursing around my head seem to be either too melodramatic, or too crude, or else woefully insufficient. Let me try it this way: I was about to be taken through a kind of portal into a raw confrontation with existence itself.

Well, that barely scratches the surface of it, but I must force myself to keep on. In so doing, I know that I must relive every moment once again, the better to describe what happened, and that in reliving every moment I risk releasing all the pain and anguish I have suppressed for so long. This is why I am hesitant. I am afraid. It may be too much for me to bear. I therefore beg some indulgence from whoever may read this. I am just an old man who tried to do his best.

# 16

Not long after we had crossed 78° North, the wind spluttered for a while, dropping away with a few final gasps and leaving us gyrating aimlessly on a calming sea. I dropped and lashed the mainsail to relieve my ears, and the boat's rig, from the constant slatting of the sail as we rolled one way then the other. In some ways, it was a pleasant break from the butting into a head sea of the previous week or two, but we were now being set south again by the current, and so risked losing many hard-won miles.

On that score, I need not have worried. A gentle zephyr soon came in from the east and with the full mainsail now restored to its rightful place aloft, we once more edged slowly northwards. The sky was as cloud-ridden as ever, the sea as pewter-grey, the air as glacial and penetrating, but this was my final moment of euphoria. With the softest of winds now caressing our starboard beam, the sea to the north was opened up once more. I sat in the hatchway, eyes fixed on the horizon ahead, as alive and as alert as I have ever felt, my heart still fizzing with anticipation.

It was round about then that the main business of this voyage started to unfold, and it began as no more than a tiny dot at the indistinct junction between the ocean and the sky. I had not seen anything quite like it at sea: there was something odd about its shape and scale and, from this distance, its apparent lack of movement. After weeks of observing nothing but the subdued and soft-edged shades of the natural world, I was jolted by the brightness of this whatever-it-was, by its garish intrusion into the all-pervading grey. I pulled out my binoculars and studied it more closely. It was orange-yellow in colour and without doubt a man-made artefact. Was it some sort of strange ship? Or was it something smaller – a scientific measurement buoy perhaps? For a while I could not decide whether it was something big a very long way away, or something small much closer. We were moving slowly towards it and I could now see that it was roughly triangular in shape. It did not seem to be moving in any direction. I unhooked the self-steering gear and took control of the tiller myself, to make sure we passed close by.

We are inquisitive creatures, we humans. We have to know everything about everything, and it was inquisitiveness that drew me towards this strange object on the sea. I wonder now whether it would have been better had I changed course and scuttled off elsewhere, ignoring this oddity, minding my own business, going my own sweet way. I had no choice, of course. It drew me towards itself like iron filings to a magnet, and in any case, I had a duty to investigate. My attraction to this object and all of the tumult that followed were as inescapable as the death now hovering near.

It soon became clear that what I was approaching was small and close, rather than large and distant, and that it was a liferaft of some sort. Yes, a liferaft, here in the far corner of the Greenland Sea. We moved closer and my mind seethed with questions and possibilities. Where the hell had it come from? Were there people in it? If so, how many? How would I cope with them with my tiny yacht? I admit, there was something thrilling about the prospect of being a rescuer. After all, what were the chances of a liferaft being found in such a remote spot? If there are people aboard, they must feel hopeless. Have they been able to set off a rescue signal of some sort? Is there a search on for them or whatever vessel they were on?

We were now just a few hundred yards away and I put all these questions out of my mind. I had to be calm and focussed to try and bring us alongside the liferaft. I lowered a panel of the sail to reduce our speed a little. In any case, the breeze was starting to strengthen, still from the east.

It was a liferaft with a canopy. As I would have to let the mainsail right out once alongside, I would have to come in on the leeward side of the raft, otherwise the boom and sheets of the mainsail might get caught up with the canopy. This meant, though, that we were likely to drift apart more quickly unless a line could be passed.

I won't dwell on the technicalities of getting a sailing yacht alongside a drifting object in what was now a rising sea. Suffice to say that it is not as easy as it may seem. I decided in fact that on the first pass I would simply sail as close as I could and try and ascertain whether there was anybody on the liferaft. So far, I had seen no sign of life: no heads appearing anywhere, no arms waving, no smoke signal.

I aimed *M.* to pass about twenty feet to windward of the raft. As we approached, I let out the mainsheet so that we were left more or less stationary, with the mainsail weather cocked to leeward, just upwind of the liferaft. The liferaft's canopy had an entry flap, secured with tapes, which was fully closed and side-on to us.

*Hello! Anybody aboard! Hello!*

There was no answer. Nothing. I tried again.

*Hello! Anybody aboard?*

We had already started to drift apart – the liferaft borne on the southerly current, while we sidled away to the west, pushed by the wind. I pulled out my binoculars again and had a close look at the raft. Above the entrance canopy I could now see a sign:

4 ЧЕЛ

*Bloody hell!*

It was a Russian liferaft. The 'ЧЕЛ' was short for ЧЕЛОВЕКА' – persons/people. Sometimes it is useful to be a Russian speaker. It was a Russian 4-man liferaft but, for the moment, showing no signs of life aboard.

I tried my previous hail in Russian. Maybe that would get a response.

*Привет! Есть-ли там кто-то?*

Nothing. Not a peep or a movement.

I was tempted to harden in the mainsail and resume my

placid passage north. It would take time and a lot of effort to backtrack and make another attempt to manoeuvre right alongside the liferaft. Why bother? If there was anybody in it, they would have responded by now.

Yes, I was tempted to sail on, and there's the nub of the matter. Had I ignored that liferaft drifting aimlessly on a frigid sea; had I overcome my inquisitiveness and continued on north, I would be a different man than the one I am today. But how can a sailor ignore a liferaft, however quiet and forlorn it seems? What, if anything, was inside it? Might its contents give a clue as to its origin? A four-man liferaft suggested that it came from a small sailing craft rather than a fishing boat or a commercial vessel, which piqued my interest even more. I knew that if I sailed on, I would soon be tormented by unanswered and unanswerable questions.

I was struck by another startling thought. My assumption that there was nobody in the liferaft might be wrong. In these waters, with a temperature close to freezing, survival times are measurable in minutes. There is a good chance that anybody having to use a liferaft might have to spend some time in the water first. Even a minute or two before getting in the liferaft might set off a fatal chain of reactions to the cold.

I groaned.

*Bloody hell!*

There was no question now that I was going to have to take a proper look. I was more than a little afraid of what I might find, and how I would cope with it, but by now I had no choice.

# 17

I made a few preparations while still hove to. I was going to have to go out on deck, a rare event, so I put on my sea boots and wet weather gear, with my harness over the top. My inviolable rule is never, ever to exit the hatch without being clipped on to the boat. I pulled out my boathook from its storage position aft, and placed it, along with a couple of coils of strong rope, in the cockpit.

It was then time to leave the haven of the cabin, as I had already decided to manage the whole manoeuvre by hand steering in the cockpit. To prepare *M.* for her sea voyages, I had reduced the cockpit's size considerably, creating a large flotation chamber at its aft end. The two narrow seats on either side had been altered to create bins for the storage of my Jordan series drogue, so I had to stand in the cockpit, or sit on the narrow bridge deck.

Having first leaned out and clipped my two harness tethers to u-bolts on the deck, I climbed up and out of the hatch – in effect a waterproof glass manhole about eighteen inches square. With all my heavy clothes and waterproofs on, it was a tight squeeze. I dropped down into the cockpit and cleared away the lines to the self-steering gear to give me free movement.

The wind was still strengthening, and seemed to be backing too, into the south-east. We had already drifted a hundred yards or so from the liferaft and occasionally I lost sight of it in the troughs now forming. I hauled in the mainsheet to get us sailing again, waited until we had built up some speed, and chose a flatter patch of water in which to go about and head back towards the orange canopy.

I knew that this time I had to be bold. The sea was rising with the wind, and if I were to have any chance of getting properly alongside the raft, and maybe even attaching a line, it had to be done now, and quickly.

One thing was in my favour. The liferaft had double flotation rings, one on top of the other, so that its sides sat quite high in the water. Conversely, *M.*, small and shapely as she is, has very modest freeboard amidships, no more than about fifteen inches. This meant that were I able to put us right alongside, it would be relatively easy for me to grab hold of the webbing attached around the upper flotation chamber of the liferaft, using either my hands or the boathook.

Sometimes it's best not to think too hard about what you are doing. With the wind and waves and current there were simply too many variables in play for me to work out the ideal approach in advance. Instead, I emptied my mind and let instinct take over. The result was that I sailed straight at the liferaft, released the mainsheet as we hit it a little way aft of our port bow, kept the tiller down as we scraped along the raft, leaned over and grabbed the strap hanging around the raft's side, and before too much pressure came on my grip, passed the end of one of my lines round the strap I was holding. Within a few seconds I had my line cleated. We were attached to the liferaft.

I could feel its weight, no doubt enhanced by the stabilising water pockets hanging down underneath it, jostling us as each wave passed. With the mainsail still up and swinging around to leeward, there was a lot of force trying to push as away from the liferaft, increasing the strain on the line connecting us. Trying to keep calm and methodical, I lowered the mainsail, lashed it firmly to its gallows and tidied up the mainsheet. I then passed a second line to the liferaft, a little further forward this time.

I was pleased to have managed everything first time, but there was one remaining problem: the canopy entrance was on the side of the liferaft facing way from us. I was going to have to turn the liferaft round if I wanted to have a look inside.

It took a while and a lot of physical effort, working the liferaft round inch by inch, using two lines attached with slippery hitches to the liferaft's straps. The routine was to slacken off the aft line a few inches, then haul in on the forward line. Next, I eased off the aft slippery hitch enough to let me slide it a few inches back towards us. Then haul in on the slack created, using the forward line. Then slacken off the forward hitch enough to move it a few inches away from us on the raft's strap. And so on. It was tortuously slow, but it kept us well-lashed and close to the liferaft, so that as far as was possible we were moving together on the waves, without too much heavy colliding.

The canopy rotated round until it was squarely facing our port side, opposite the forward end of the cockpit. I resisted the temptation to start opening it until it was in the best possible position, and until I had both my lines taut and well cleated.

In any case, I needed a few moments to recover after the efforts of the previous half hour or so; this was the first real physical exertion of the voyage. Moreover, I was still adjusting to the insecurity I felt out on deck. I was acutely aware that should I go overboard for any reason, even if attached to the ship, that I would be unlikely to survive.

I admit, too, that I was in no hurry to find out what was inside the liferaft. I could now see that the tapes of the canopy entrance had been knotted shut from the inside rather than the outside. Logically, that meant that there must be at least one person aboard. I had still not heard any sound or movement. It seemed inevitable that I was going to find at least one dead person when I opened the tapes. Despite my years, death was still an almost completely foreign country to me. I did not welcome having to meet it, especially alone and in such a desolate spot. I went to sea to observe and celebrate life, not to confront its antithesis.

# 18

I leaned inside the open hatch and grabbed my rigging knife from its hook to starboard. The only way I could reach the knotted tapes of the canopy, or the lower ones anyway, was by leaning out from the side deck with my body hanging over *M.'s* single lifeline. In such a precarious position it would be impossible to use both hands – one was needed for hanging onto the lifeline as I leaned out. I would simply cut whichever tapes I could reach with my knife. I made sure that my harness was tethered to two attachment points and positioned my feet as comfortably as I could on the side deck. In fact, there was virtually no side deck to squat on, as most of its narrow width was taken by the oar stowed along its length. Feet splayed, I jammed my toes under the oar, held tight to the lifeline with my left hand and leaned out as far as I could, right arm extended, open knife in hand.

The lines with which I had attached us to the liferaft were still taut and so, despite the motion, I was able to pass my knife through the gap between the two sides of the entry flap and saw downwards, cutting the tapes.

The orange material of the flap was now hanging down vertically, rather than at the angle of the canopy, creating a gap at its base, through which I could partially see inside the raft. It was dark in there, but I could make out a pair of rubber sea-boots close to the bottom of the flap.

*Oh no! No, no, no!*

I retrieved the boathook and used it to lift the flap a little more.

All my worst fears were confirmed. There was a body lying there: just one person, not very big, curled into a foetal position.

*Oh God! What the hell do I do now?*

For a few moments I could not move. It was a paralysis brought on by too many conflicting thoughts and emotions. One half of me wanted to release the lines holding the liferaft, there and then, to reset our course northwards, to resume the voyage just as it had been, to re-establish my harmonious solitude, to forget this nonsense with Russian liferafts and dead bodies. The other half of me knew that this was impossible, that the inexorable grind of cause and effect was inescapable, that the wheels turning implacably towards whatever was going to happen were now too set in their motion for any halt or reversal.

Yes, for a few moments I was paralysed as I slowly accepted the inevitable: my voyage as it had been conceived was over. My enterprise had been transformed, in just a few minutes, into something quite new and unimaginable. I had to jettison a year's worth of planning and preparation and give myself up to whatever ghastly tale was now about to unfold.

This mental turmoil was not enough to stop a wry thought crossing my mind. Had we crossed 78° North as originally intended, in 10° West longitude, we would have passed well to the west of this liferaft. I would never have seen it. I did not know then, and I do not know even now, whether that would have been for better or for worse. The machinations of fate lie well beyond the judgement of mortals.

*

These abstractions sped through my brain in a millisecond, to be replaced by a more immediate and terrifying realization: I was going to have to get myself aboard the liferaft. Whoever was lying there looked lifeless, but I had to be sure before deciding what to do next.

The prospect of having to step off my little yacht and transfer myself into the liferaft filled me with a cold dread. I had never, ever left any of my yachts when at sea. The cabin was my haven. Being on deck, especially in heavy weather, could be disconcerting. To wilfully go over the side had always been, until this moment, an unthinkable prospect.

I was wearing my harness, but the rope tethers that I clipped to attachment points on the deck were not long enough to reach inside the liferaft. I tied a bowline in the unused end of one of the warps I had used to lash us to the raft and clipped both the carabiners at the end of my tethers over the loop. It was a highly unsatisfactory arrangement, but it at least meant that I was still attached to *M.*. I worked my way to the aft of the cockpit and undid the lashing that secured the lifeline, the wire that runs around the side of the yacht a couple of feet above the deck, to the pushpit. I did not want to have to step over this wire when transferring from one craft to the other; it would be physically awkward and keep my centre of gravity too high. I pulled the lifeline forward as far as it would go through its hole in the top of the aftermost stanchion, thereby leaving a clear route on and off the liferaft.

All this time, the sea had been building as it adapted to the stronger south-easterly. This higher sea was starting to accentuate the disparities between the two craft lashed together. Our union with the liferaft was becoming more fraught. The previous harmony of our movement on the waves was giving way to a more fractious connection. I could sense that the two vessels were trying to tear themselves apart from each other as each wave passed under us.

Hanging over the side of the liferaft, beneath the canopy entrance, were two parallel tapes, about fifteen inches apart, which I assumed were the top part of a webbing ladder that somebody in the water could use to climb into the raft. I leaned out and grabbed the top of these two tapes, one in each hand, and when the moment seemed right, pushed off with my left leg while throwing my right leg over the upper buoyancy ring. For a second or two I sat astride the ring, not well balanced, until a sudden lurch threw me through the canopy entrance. As I fell into the liferaft my head scraped against the top of the entrance, ripping my waterproof hat off my head and pulling it over my eyes. Luckily, I did not fall onto the body lying there.

Even before I had had the time to readjust my hat, I was almost retching from the smell inside the liferaft.

*Oh God!*

At first, I thought it must be the odour of death, of decomposing flesh, but after a second or two I realised that it was something more vital and familiar: the air inside the liferaft was rank with the smell of urine and, much worse still, faeces.

*

In commencing this narrative, I reminded myself that my duty is to look, see and tell. I am determined to relate what happened on this voyage as directly and as fully as I am able. This includes the many aspects of the tale which are unpleasant or distasteful. There are plenty more to come and so I am starting as I mean to go on. Nothing will be omitted. That is the pledge I have made to myself, as any censorship, or toning down, of the true facts of the matter would be a betrayal. I make no apology for this. Without the truth this story is worthless.

*

I instinctively leaned my head towards the canopy opening to get a lungful of fresher air, pulling my hat down firmly at the same time. I could now see *M.* rolling wildly alongside, secured to the liferaft by just those two hastily arranged lines.

*Bloody hell!*

It was the first time in half a century of ocean sailing that, on the open sea, I had seen a boat of mine from any vantage point other than on board. I had never left the mother ship, had never wanted to, and now felt a momentary surge of terror at being separated from her. Under my knees the cold floor of the liferaft jiggled and undulated. The attachment lines strained and snatched as each wave passed underneath. I felt sure that the liferaft was going to break away at any moment, leaving me adrift on a frigid sea with nothing but a corpse for company.

*Jesus Christ!*

The urge to abandon the raft as quickly as possible and get back on board was almost too much to resist. I gave myself just a few seconds to check the body. It was wearing the blue seaboots I had seen, yellow waterproofs, a Russian shapka with the flaps down, and was curled up on its righthand side, head hidden under its left arm. I pulled at the body's left shoulder to roll it over onto its back.

*Jesus!*

The head flopped over onto the floor of the liferaft and just for a fraction of a second its eyelids opened, revealing two cornflower blue eyes. Under the shapka these eyes were framed by a straggle of blonde curls. The eyes closed again and I heard, I think, just the faintest murmur from the body's half open mouth.

*Bloody hell!*

It was a woman, and she seemed to be still alive. I had expected a dead Russian bear, an unshaven and square-jawed bruiser. Instead, here was a living twenty-something with a face which, although disfigured by stress and cold, would not have been out of place in a ballroom scene from *Anna Karenina*.

*Oh God!*

I had to get back on board my ship. The two vessels were rolling and jostling frenetically, and I was now quite convinced they would break apart any second. I had to move, and quickly. There was only one thing I could do. I would have to take the girl with me.

Ha! Words easily thought and easily written, but not quite so straightforward in the reality. How the hell was I going to shift a lifeless deadweight of maybe a hundred and ten or a hundred and twenty pounds, from inside the liferaft, onto *M.'s* deck, and then down the hatchway into the cabin? I had no idea. I'd just have to do the best I could. My fear was that in trying to make the crossing back on board, I would either drop the girl's body, or my body, or both of our bodies, into the sea.

I have always been uncompromising about keeping things, everything, attached when on deck. It was a lesson I first had drummed into me as an able seaman on a square rigger more than fifty years previously. Working aloft, every tool you carried and used had to be attached to a line in some way. A spanner or a rigging knife dropped accidentally could easily kill or maim somebody on deck eighty feet below.

I was still attached to the mother ship by the line I had rigged, unsatisfactory though it was. I had to find some way of securing the girl's body. I realised that she was wearing a harness – a good one with straps under the crotch. I still had plenty of slack on the line attaching me to *M..* I untied the bowline I had made and pushed the end of the line under one shoulder strap of her harness, then under the other shoulder strap, then led the rope round the same way once again for good measure. She was now secured to the line by two loops under her harness. There was enough rope left for me to make another bowline on which I re-attached my two tethers. All in all, it was as un-seamanlike as you could get, but I had it done in twenty seconds; I no longer had time for anything fancy.

As with coming alongside the liferaft, I threw myself without too much forethought into the task of getting us both aboard *M.*. I dragged the girl's body from where it was lying into a position where it was leaning against the upper buoyancy ring. Kneeling on the ring, one knee on each side of her head, I reached over and grabbed the base of a lifeline stanchion, brought my feet up to the ring and launched myself over the gap. I landed awkwardly on the side deck, giving my left knee an agonising blow on the oar lashed there.

Well, I had to forget that and somehow get the girl aboard. I now had two ropes to haul on: the line cleated aboard that was now attached by the two loops to the shoulder straps of her harness, plus the end of the same line that was attached to my tethers.

It was all or nothing. I stood up on the deck of the flotation chamber at the aft end of *M.'s* cockpit, to give me some height and some leverage. With the two lines now taut and married together in my gloved hands I simply hauled her up and over the raft's buoyancy ring, leaning back to move her a bit at a time, then inching my hands one at a time down the lines to take in the slack. She was now half out of the liferaft, with her knees over the inside of the buoyancy ring and her torso flopping back towards me. Fearing she might slip right out of the raft if I hesitated at all, I took a quick step back, arranging my feet on each side of the tiller, and hauled as hard and as quickly as I possibly could. With this one desperate effort I pulled her across the from the liferaft until the top third of her body was lying across the side deck and cockpit coaming, and her legs were stretched over to the buoyancy ring, on which her seaboots were now resting.

Thinking I had done the hard work, I paused for a moment to get my breath. A steep wave passed underneath. With a ripping, popping sound, one of the fittings attaching the webbing that I had initially lashed us to parted company with the liferaft, slackening off the lashing and opening up a gap between the two vessels. Extra strain came onto the adjoining fitting and that went too, further widening the gap. The girl's feet fell off the buoyancy ring, which was now six or seven feet away and crumpling rapidly as it deflated. Her legs fell into the sea and she started to slide off the side deck, encouraged by a particularly severe roll of the yacht.

*No! No! No!*

I braced as hard as I could, my back now against the after end of the lashed sail bundle, and with three almighty heaves got her aboard. I couldn't lay her torso right down as she would have been lying across the tiller, with the risk of damaging both it and her. Still keeping her torso upright, I worked her forward until I was standing on the narrow bridge deck just aft of the hatch.

I was exhausted and breathing heavily, but I had to carry on: there was simply nowhere on deck where I could comfortably stretch out her body. I just had to find enough strength for the final and perhaps most difficult manoeuvre – lowering her safely down the hatch.

I grabbed her round her upper back with my left arm and picked her up with my right arm under her knees.

*Bloody hell!*

She was not too heavy, but it was all I could do to keep myself from tumbling over, what with the roll of the yacht and this weight in my arms. I managed to manoeuvre her sea boots through the hatch and let her legs drop down. I lowered her until she was sitting on the edge of the hatch and once more got hold of the lines from each shoulder strap. Keeping the tension on these lines, so that her torso was still upright, I stood up again and lifted her off the side of the hatch until her body was hanging straight down, half of it through the hatch, then, using the ropes, lowered her down. I knew that she would end up in an awkward position, with her legs buckling underneath her, but I could not be arranging her down below while lowering her down from above.

*I'm sorry! I'm sorry!*

Even though the girl was not conscious, I felt I was hurting her as I lowered her down willy-nilly, like a sack of potatoes. With her torso now taking up most of the space in the hatchway, I could not see what was going on with her legs and feet, and therefore how she was likely to end up on the cabin sole. I just lowered her down as gently as I could, hoping she would naturally adopt a position that was not too contorted or dangerous. As I lowered, I could feel her upper body bending forward. When there was no more tension on the ropes, I stuck my head in the hatch to see what was going on. She was lying prone on the cabin sole, more or less face down, her knees bent and her feet splayed awkwardly on the lowest rung of the companionway ladder. It could have been a lot worse.

# 19

It was with the best of intentions that I began the task of telling this untold story. I owed it to both myself and the world to reveal the secrets of this voyage. Whispering like a penitent into the ear of the priest, I thought that this retelling might ease the burden I have been carrying for so long, but now I am not so sure. As I cast my mind back and replay every little detail of what took place, far from becoming lighter, the burden grows heavier and more intense. This supposed expiation is becoming yet another punishment. I have had to force myself once more to see that half-dead body spread-eagled like a ragdoll flung carelessly through the hatch. Yes, I had tried my best to be gentle, and even now I cannot see how I could have done things any differently, but it wrenches at my heart to see once again such a stark image of that poor girl's helplessness. It was at that moment, too, that I understood, properly and for the first time, the enormity of what was happening. I had a fragile life on my hands. That life, about which I knew nothing, was now my responsibility. A young woman, whom I presumed to be Russian, who had a past and an imagined future fleshed out with the usual hopes and dreams, who had parents and maybe brothers and sisters, friends and lovers and colleagues, who had, in a word, an *existence,* was now lying unconscious on the cabin sole of my little yacht, rolling to the motion of the waves in the most outlandish corner of the Greenland Sea, and the only person who could help her was I, an aging singlehanded sailor with a leaning towards solitude and the scantiest of medical knowledge.

Yes, I have a strong urge to stop right now. I should delete this file, once and for all, just as I flung my logbooks overboard and deleted all my photographs. The reliving of this story is already becoming painful, almost unbearably so, but it has hardly commenced. If I am finding it difficult to continue at this early juncture, how will things be as we progress into the dark heart of the matter?

I am not sure, then, that I have it in me to see this task through to its conclusion, but I will try. I will try, and as I have already said, I will hide nothing, however upsetting this may be to any reader of delicate sensibilities.

# 20

I was now faced with three conflicting priorities, such that for a second or two I dithered, working out the best order to do things. Clearly, I had to attend to the girl, but *M.* was rolling increasingly violently, lying as she was beam on to what was now a strong sea. I had to get some sail up and settle us to a comfortable point of sailing. Worse than that, we were still attached to the liferaft, and with it no longer lying taut alongside, it was careering around to windward, in its half-crumpled state, and was threatening to drift around our stern and get caught up with our self-steering gear.

I made my decision: liferaft, girl, raise sail. Reaching down inside the hatch, I disconnected my tethers from the rope attached to the girl's harness and re-attached them to two suitable points on deck. I hauled in on the lines attaching us to the raft. This was hard work, with the liferaft less buoyant and giving less support to the heavy water pockets underneath. I was glad I had secured the lines with slippery hitches, as they could be released simply by pulling on the end of each hitch's final loop. The original hitches had tightened considerably around the tapes they were tied to, what with the tension they had been under for quite a while now, but a sharp tug released each loop. *M.* was fore-reaching very slightly, no doubt propelled by the sail bundle, and we eased away from the liferaft. I was glad to see the back of it. I really needed to re-attach the lifeline I had disconnected, but that could wait. I had to go below and attend to the body lying there.

I stepped through the hatch and slowly descended the companionway ladder. The girl's feet were still on the lowest step. I twisted round in the hatchway until I was facing forward, ducked my head under the cabin top and placed each foot carefully on the cabin sole, one each side of her legs. My two feet and her two legs took up pretty much the whole width of the sole. From there I bent forward and for the second time that day, rolled the girl over onto her back. Her eyes were closed, and she seemed to be shivering. Well, that meant that at least she was still alive. I took a good hold of the shoulder straps of her harness, one in each hand, and pulled her up until her head was level with my chin. Quickly stepping my right foot over her legs, I laid her torso down on the starboard berth, her head facing towards the bow, bent down and with my right hand picked up her legs under her knees and placed them on the berth too.

*Bloody hell!*

A stream of sea water, the result of her quick dunking, flowed from each boot as I raised her legs up, spreading over the mattress top and running down onto the cabin sole.

I grabbed a towel and dabbed at the bunk top, then straightened her out as best I could, before locating the two sets of straps I use to lash myself to the berth in heavy weather, and which are tucked away under the berth mattress when not in use. I tied her to the bunk, with one set of straps across her upper chest, the other across her thighs. Her head was still flopping around somewhat each time *M.* rolled, so I tried to limit the movement with a pillow and a bag of clothes.

I just wanted to see her at some sort of ease. It had been a brutal journey for her from the floor of the liferaft to my bunk. She had been pushed and pulled around, dragged across hard, uneven surfaces, half dropped into the sea, raised and lowered, all in the roughest way. I had no doubt she was badly bruised from the manhandling.

The air in the cabin was by now rank with the smell of the girl's urine and faeces. My mind was already ranging ahead with thought about how I was going to cope with this problem, and for the moment I avoided the obvious answer - I had not yet adjusted in any way to all the implications of the situation. I did not then know it, but I was still at the very lowest point of a steep learning curve.

With the girl now laid out on my bunk as comfortably as I could manage, for the moment at least, I rotated the chart table round on its swivel, to give access the single burner alcohol stove underneath. My cooking pan lives permanently on the stove, kept in place in all weathers by two clamps. I took the empty pan off the stove and stowed it in the locker underneath, then lit the stove, adjusting it to a low heat.

*

I have very little medical knowledge, but it seemed clear to me that the girl was hypothermic: her body temperature had dropped to a dangerously low level. I knew that the cold hereabouts could kill very quickly – anybody fully immersed in the sea will only last a few minutes. I remembered a report from the UK Marine Accident Board about man overboard incidents, which had shocked me. Half of those who go overboard, even on fully manned vessels, do not survive. Even in the warmer waters around the UK, anybody who goes overboard becomes unresponsive after about eleven minutes. All this seemed to suggest that the girl had stepped off whatever vessel she was on straight into the liferaft, without spending any time in the water. Had she been immersed in the sea before climbing into the liferaft, she would almost certainly be dead by now.

I searched my mind for what I knew about hypothermia and how to treat it. Only a few vague recollections came to mind. Something about not trying to reheat the body too aggressively. I seemed to recall that you shouldn't rub somebody who was hypothermic to try to stimulate the blood flow. That was the full extent of my knowledge, and even that I wasn't sure about.

Well, if I were to save the girl, a good way to start would be to heat up the cabin. It has a very small air space, is almost completely insulated, and therefore warms up quickly and retains the heat reasonably well. The only form of heating I had on board was the little stove, which I only ever used twice a day, and which was adequate even in the high Arctic. Even on a low setting, the stove would soon raise the cabin temperature considerably.

*

In the meantime, I had to attend to the ship. We were drifting aimlessly, with the deck a complete mess. I exited the hatch, closed it behind me to keep the heat in, and attacked the cat's cradle of lines created by our encounter with the liferaft. I re-attached and re-tensioned the lifeline I had released, set up once more the five control lines for the self-steering gear, and re-coiled the ropes used to moor us to the liferaft, before dropping them down the hatch onto the cabin sole. As I did so, I had a quick look at my passenger. She was still lying completely inert, eyes closed.

I unlashed the sail bundle and folded the tubular boom gallows forward so that they were lying on the cabin top. A final look around confirmed that everything was once more in good order. It was time to set sail.

While working, I had been considering what to do. In fact, there was not much choice. I had to head for the nearest accessible settlement, to get help for the girl, and that was Longyearbyen, on Svalbard, three hundred miles to our east. With the wind currently in the south-east, it would be a slog. The girl's bunk would also be on the windward side, adding to the discomfort. Well, the wind was unlikely to hold for too long. We just had to get on with it.

With the lines to the self-steering back in place, it was easier for me to manage things from the hatch from here on. The hatch was now open, but with my body blocking most of the opening, very little heat was escaping from the cabin. I hauled up two panels of the mainsail, threw off the tiller lashings, set the windvane to 40° to the apparent wind and attached the self-steering chain to the tiller.

What a joy it was to settle once more to purposeful movement through the water, to feel the heel and thrust of the hull into the waves, to hear the sea creaming once more under our lee. For a few seconds I sat in the hatchway, enjoying the sensuality of the moment. It was almost as if nothing had changed, as if I could still roam free in careless solitude.

I took a last look at the robust sea now running, checked the horizons for any hazards, and once more dropped below, closing the hatch behind me.

# 21

This was the moment I had been dreading. Thus far, I had been able to distract myself with all the necessary demands of sailoring, but now we were settled on a course, with the ship taking care of herself, there was nothing to keep me from attending properly to the girl.

I knew what I was going to have to do, and I did not want to do it. I was not even sure I would be able to do it.

The combination of the unaccustomed heat in the cabin, along with the stench from the girl, was almost unbearable. I had to fight the urge to stick my head out of the hatch to breathe some pure, cool air. Forcing myself to get a grip on my revulsion, I set to work.

For the first time, I looked closely at my new passenger's face. The taut blue skin and pale lips gave her a deathly look but did not mask the regularity and beauty of her features. I took off my right glove and placed my hand on her left cheek, caressing her very gently and hoping for some kind of reaction.

*Hello? You're safe now. My name's Roger. Hello?*

Nothing. Her shallow, rapid breathing continued to the same rhythm. Her eyes stayed shut.

I tried again in Russian. Was there a slight flicker of her eyelids, or did I imagine it? I carried on in English, for myself as much as for her.

*I'm really sorry, but I'm going to have to clean you up and get you into some warm dry clothes. You'll feel much better. I'm sorry, but it has to be done. I'll be as quick as I can.*

I rummaged in the bags of clothes at the aft end of the port quarter berth, pulling out some used tee-shirts, some clean woollen underwear, tracksuit bottoms, socks and a heavy woollen sweater. I also retrieved a couple of clean towels.

It seemed sensible to start at the lower end, but first I had to take off her harness. I released the buckles, slid the shoulder straps down and under the bunk strap across her chest and just kept going, pulling the harness down, under the lower bunk strap and over her ankles until it came free.

I took off my gloves, unlashed the straps across her thighs and pulled off her right sea boot. I suspected there might still be some water in there, so I kept it as upright as possible, jamming it under the lowest companionway step. I did the same with her left boot. She was wearing thick blue woollen socks, both sodden with cold seawater. I pulled off the socks, held them in one hand, quickly opened the hatch with the other hand and dropped them into the cockpit.

*OK. Let's give those feet a quick dry…*

I wrapped a towel around both of her feet to dry them off,

squeezing the towel gently. I took the towel off her right foot and held the foot between my hands. It was deathly cold. Her toenails were decorated with chipped sky-blue nail varnish. I would have liked to have held that foot between my hands long enough to transfer some warmth into it, but there were too many other things to attend to. I had to try and save a whole body, not just a foot.

She was wearing yellow waterproof trousers, elasticated at the waist, which I worked down over her legs and pulled off. I folded them roughly and stuffed them into a bag for used clothing. The trousers stank and I would have liked to throw them in the cockpit, but they might be needed again.

Under the waterproof trousers was a pair of black padded ski pants. They were made of synthetic material of some sort and were quite damp. They were also bibbed, like overalls, and to get them off I first had to take off her waterproof jacket. I re-lashed the lower straps and undid the straps round her chest. Tied in this way she was much more unstable. In each heavy roll, her torso was sliding off the smooth mattress top, forcing me to stop what I was doing and catch her before she fell onto the cabin sole. I worked her jacket off. Under the jacket was a heavy dark-grey fleece which I had not noticed before. I pulled that over her head and off her arms as best I could.

*Sorry! Sorry!*

The fleece was cold and damp, although not wringing wet. I had turned it inside out when pulling it off, exposing the label. I had a quick look. I can't remember the make, Sivera perhaps, but at the bottom of the label was printed:

### *Сделанно в России*

*Made in Russia.* Well, no surprises there.

I threw the fleece onto the pile of bags on the port quarter berth and started on the ski pants. I knew I had to work quickly. The cabin was now very warm, to the extent that I considered turning off the stove, but it seemed wise to wait until I had her cleaned and in dry clothes first.

I pulled the straps of the bib off her shoulders and worked the top of the pants down to her waist. Under the bib she was wearing a woollen checked shirt. Before going any further, I grabbed a couple of the used tee-shirts I had pulled out and spread them out on the bunk underneath her midriff and legs.

By now I was working in a kind of white heat. I had found a rhythm, my head was clear, I knew what had to be done. It was the frenzy of the moment that kept me going. I was now engaged in something so unthinkable that I may as well have been living in another dimension. Yes, I know, there are people who do this sort of thing every day – carers and nurses and ambulance drivers and A & E medics and funeral directors and so on - and I salute them. They would probably find my reaction to the situation I was in quite exaggerated, or pitiful, or even comical. *Yes, sunshine, this is what life is really like! Where the hell have you been all these years?* Well, it's an aspect of life that had somehow passed me by for over seven decades. I was now catching up in double-quick time.

# 22

On re-reading the chapter that I have just written, I realise that I somehow left out a couple of important details. I am not sure how they were missed. It could be that my memory is failing, or it could be that however hard I am working to recount everything just as it happened, my mind is still being selective. Perhaps there are some things that my inner psyche does not want to recall, for reasons best known to itself. The workings of the subconscious mind are by definition beyond comprehension.

Anyway, I realise now that I forgot to mention the girl's hands. Her waterproof jacket had the usual kind of elasticated cuffs, so I had to take off the girl's gloves before I could slide her hands through these cuffs. The gloves were thickly padded and seemed to be waterproof, as her hands were quite dry. Like her feet, her hands were blue and icy cold, but with unvarnished, well-manicured nails. What struck me was how small her hands were, and how delicate. My own hands are big, broad hams, misshapen and scarred from a lifetime of hard use. I had trouble imagining the girl's hands hauling on a halyard or doing the usual sailorly things. Perhaps this impression was enhanced by them being so lifeless. Maybe, once they were again coursing with hot blood, they would re-assume an aura of strength and vitality. At that moment, however, something about those hands touched me to the core. There was a terrible pathos bound up in their frozen fragility. I had forgotten about those hands and now that I think about them once more, I feel an inexplicable sadness.

I had also forgotten that I had taken off the girl's shapka before pulling her fleece over her head. Unlike mine, this shapka was made of real fur. I undid the bow tied under her chin that was holding the flaps down over her ears and gently pulled off the hat from the top. An unruly mess of straw-coloured hair fell onto the bunk mattress. I guess that the hair was about shoulder length, perhaps slightly less. I felt inside the hat to see if there was any warmth there. It was dry, but almost as cold as the girl's hands and feet.

*Bloody hell!*

As yet, there was no sign whatsoever that the girl was warming up or reviving. I remember now that, before pulling her fleece over her head, I had held the girl's head in my hands for a brief moment, feeling the softness of her hair under my palms. I had spoken once more to the girl.

*Привет! Кто ты? Пожалуйста, проснись! Hello! Who are you? Please wake up!*

Bent over her, with her head cradled in my hands, I had

stared at her face, trying to find some sign of a response, but there was nothing. No movement of her eyelids, no change in her half-open lips, no break in the almost imperceptible rhythm of her breathing.

Yes, I had forgotten the first sight of her hands and the feel of her hair under my rough old palms. Or perhaps not forgotten, but pushed aside, the better to spare myself the pain of the memories.

# 23

I continued on with what I had to do; there was simply no avoiding it. I eased her ski pants over her narrow hips and worked them down to her feet, all the while trying to keep the tee-shirts I had laid out under her in place. For the moment I dropped the pants onto the cabin sole, forcing myself to ignore their ghastly smell.

Under the ski pants she was wearing black thermal tights of some artificial material. I stripped them off as quickly as I could and dropped them on top of the ski pants. All that was left on the lower half of the girl was a pair of black panties.

From here on I worked as quickly as I could. The poor girl was exposed in every way and I wanted her covered up and warm as soon as possible, but before that I had to get her clean and fresh smelling. I was embarrassed for her and embarrassed for myself. What if she were to wake up right at this moment?

What if she were to open her eyes and see that she had been stripped almost naked by a complete stranger? What if she were to realise that she was the cause of the now overpowering smell of bodily waste?

I pulled my pan out of its locker, put it back on the stove and half filled it with water from the water bottle I always keep near the companionway steps, then pulled another used tee-shirt out of a bag and put it on the bunk near her feet. Finally, I opened the hatch quickly and pulled in my toilet bucket from the cockpit, where it is always attached by a long line, before dropping the hatch lid down.

I spoke to the girl, again to comfort myself as much as her.

*Прости. Прости. Мне обязательно надо это сделать. У меня нет выбора. I'm sorry. I'm sorry. I really have to do this. I don't have a choice.*

I untied the bunk strap over her thighs and spread her legs slightly. Working carefully, I eased her panties down, alternately from the top and the bottom, doing my best not to spill their noxious contents. At some stage during whatever ordeal she had been through, she had had a loose bowel movement. It was impossible to keep everything contained, especially during the delicate operation of pulling each foot through. Bunching the top and sides of the panties together to hold what remained, I dropped the whole bundle into my toilet bucket. Despite my care, there was soil everywhere: on her upper thighs, along her legs, on the tee-shirts underneath her.

I took the tee-shirt I had placed near her feet and used to it give her an initial clean-up.

*I'm sorry! I have to do it!*

I wiped around her crotch and bottom as carefully as I

could, trying to keep the now dirty tee-shirt well away from her vagina. She was unshaven, making the cleaning somewhat more challenging. I folded and refolded the tee-shirt to create new clean patches and worked my way down her legs, wiping away all the spills from her panties. When the tee-shirt was no longer serviceable, I dropped it in the toilet bucket and took a few squares of the kitchen roll I keep on a shelf above the stove. I used this for a more delicate cleaning around her pubic area, throwing each sheet into the toilet bucket as soon as it had been used.

There were still a couple of soiled tee-shirts spread under her legs, but I left these for the moment. The water in the pan on the stove was now warm. I turned off the flame completely for the first time since bringing the girl aboard, as I did not want the water to get any hotter and there was nowhere I could keep the pan apart from on the stove top. I retrieved my toilet bag from its shelf and pulled out a flannel and a bar of soap. I checked that the water in the pan was not too hot, soaked the flannel for a few seconds, partially wrung it out and rubbed some soap on it.

*

How can this be? How can a man be sailing calmly along, all alone on a distant sea, and within scarcely an hour find himself making the most intimate of ministrations to a woman he has never before met, whose name he does not know, with whom he has not exchanged a single meaningful word, and for whose life he now has total responsibility?

To that I would add another question. How can it be

that I could feel such tenderness for this inert body spread-eagled on my bunk? Here was one of Lucian Freud's more uncompromising portraits lifted off the canvas and made raw and naked flesh, right here in my tiny cabin. Here, life was imitating art and trumping it a thousand times. The two dimensions of the canvas had become not just three, but four or five or more. To the visual intensity of the tableau laid out before me was added a physical maelstrom of cold and heat and odour, along with the emotional and metaphysical turmoil of doubt, guilt, worry and sheer incomprehension of what was going on. And all of that was overlaid with this most unexpected reaction: a brotherly affection for this woman. She had not, of course, chosen me to look after her. That was down to pure chance, but she was here, and totally dependent on me. It was as if she really had chosen me, and for that I was both touched and honoured.

*Я сделаю для тебя всё что в моих силах. Обещаю. I will do everything I can for you. I promise.*

I should add that I felt absolutely no lust for this girl, not the least physical arousal. Not because she was not attractive, but because the situation was so extreme, so far removed from the mundanely sexual, so desperate, that there was simply no foundation on which any erotic fantasy could be erected.

*

I started cleaning her with the soaped cloth. Rather than wringing it out in my sole cooking pan, I held the pan over my toilet bucket and poured warm water from it over the cloth while giving it a good squeeze. After a few goings-over with the cloth, I pulled the soiled and damp tee-shirts from under her and threw them into the toilet bucket. I then made a final pass over her crotch and bottom and legs. She was now as clean as I could make her under the circumstances. She was probably more sweet-smelling too, but that was still masked by the pungent smell from the toilet bucket.

Apart from my own bodily waste, it is my golden rule never to throw anything in the sea. For once, I broke that rule. I opened the hatch, lifted the toilet bucket out, over my head, and climbed up the companionway. With one mighty heave I threw the accumulated mass of soiled clothes over the lee side. I dipped the bucket in the sea a couple of times, retrieving it with its permanently attached line, and gave it a quick scrub with the brush kept for that purpose in the cockpit.

I ducked back inside the cabin but did not close the hatch entirely. I was desperate to rid the cabin of its foul-smelling air. I opened the port-light at the aft end of the cabin roof as far it would go, to encourage a draught, relit the stove and put another pan of water over the flame. Then it was back to the girl.

I ran a towel over the parts I had cleaned to make sure she was dry, dabbing gently. It was tempting to rub hard, to try to stimulate some blood flow, but as I said, I had a vague memory that this was not advised for hypothermia. I then worked a clean pair of my long merino-wool long johns up her legs to her waist. They were of course far too big, but it was the best I could do. These were followed by clean tracksuit bottoms and a clean pair of thick woollen socks. I laid a heavy blanket, doubled, over her waist and legs and retied the bunk straps over her thighs.

*Это лучше, не правда ли? That's better, isn't it?*

The worst of the job was now done, but I still had her top half to think about. I felt the check shirt she still had on. It had an unpleasant damp feel to it. Sticking out from under the bottom of her shirt was the hem of a black thermal vest of the same material as her tights, it too damp.

*Bugger!*

I would have preferred to have wrapped her up in blankets just as she was, but her upper clothes had the sticky feel of sea water and so were unlikely to dry out.

*Извини пожалуйста. Я ещё не закончил. I'm sorry. I haven't quite finished.*

I undid the bunk strap across her chest, unbuttoned her shirt front and cuffs and worked it up her back, over her head and off her arms. Around her right wrist there was an identity bracelet – a gold chain attached to a plate with a name inscribed on it in Cyrillic script:

*Ларочка*

Lárochka.

Lárochka! So that's who you are! Lárochka!

*Ларочка! Добро пожаловать на борт, Ларочка! Lárochka! Welcome aboard, Lárochka!*

I knew that Lárochka could be her proper given name, or that it could also be a diminutive, an affectionate form, of which the Russians are so fond, for Larissa, or even Lara.

My relationship with the girl, the way I thought about her, was instantly transformed. She was no longer an empty canvas. I had something to grasp on to. A humanising name, an identity. Lárochka!

I leaned over her face. Nothing had changed since the last time I had looked at her closely.

*Ну, Ларочка. Очень рад познакомиться. Well, Lárochka. I'm very pleased to meet you.*

I moved my mouth closer to her ear.

*Ларочка...Ларочка. Всё будет в порядке. Обещаю. Lárochka...Lárochka. Everything will be OK. I promise.*

The vest underneath her shirt was long-sleeved and tight. I tried to work it off her as gently as I could, but it was impossible without contorting her arms and head beyond what was reasonable. I took my scissors from the rack over the stove and cut the vest up the front and down each sleeve. I could then pull the whole thing off her from underneath her back.

On the girl's right upper arm there was a small tattoo. At first, I thought it was a swallow, but looking at it more closely I realised that it was in fact an Arctic tern, its long wings raised high, and its tail feathers spread in a wide V. The bird, one of my favourite seabirds, was depicted in simple, unfussy lines. Under the Arctic tern there was a scroll, on which was inscribed the word *Свобода. Freedom.*

She was wearing a black bra. I felt the material at the base of the front straps. Cold and damp. I covered her upper body with a thick towel and reached under her back to undo the bra clasp. I peeled away the bra and patted the towel all over her torso to make sure she was dry. A clean woollen thermal vest was lying on the forward end of the quarter berth. The fact that it was much too big for her made it easy to put on. I threaded her arms through the sleeves then pulled the neck opening over her head. To make her even more snug, it seemed a good idea to pull the waistband of the long johns as high as it would go and tuck the vest into it.

My most treasured item of clothing aboard, that I kept in reserve for the coldest weather in the High Arctic, was a woollen fisherman's sweater knitted in the Faroes. Thus far on this voyage, it had not been called into service, and now seemed the appropriate moment. It had a high roll neck and an appropriately Nordic pattern. Like the thermal vest, it was easy to thread over her arms and head. It suited the girl's blonde hair and delicate features perfectly and for a brief second the pathos of the moment, the beauty of this human being – Lárochka, hovering between life and death, stabbed at my heart.

# 24

The air in the cabin was by now somewhat fresher, so I closed the hatch properly and left the aft portlight slightly ajar. The water on the stove had started to steam. I took a couple of empty one-litre water bottles from the forepeak locker and, using a funnel, filled each one about three-quarters full with hot water. Each of these was then wrapped in a tea towel and tucked under her sweater on each side of her torso.

I worked her gloves back over her limp fingers as best I could and threaded her feet into the moonboots I usually wear below in the Arctic. I would have to make do with my ordinary seaboots. Lifting her head gently, I pulled her fur shapka over her tousle of blonde hair and tied the flaps under her chin. Her eyelids flickered just once, almost imperceptibly. I spoke softly to her.

*Ларочка... оставай сильной... всё будет хорошо. Lárochka... stay strong... everything will be fine.*

I untied both the bunk straps, unfolded the blanket over her legs and covered her up to her chin with it. Over that I laid my unzipped sleeping bag, then retied the bunk straps. For the moment there was nothing more I could do. She was clean, dry, and as warm and comfortable as I could make her.

I was by now exhausted and hungry, but I had to attend to the ship. During the previous half hour or so, while working on Lárochka, I had been aware that the wind was backing, bringing us round into a head sea. We were now pitching heavily and occasionally stalling.

I opened the hatch and surveyed the scene. The sea was growing angry, with a strengthening southerly wind blowing obliquely across a wave train still running from the south-east. The cloud cover seemed lower and more oppressive. The one consolation was that this wind gave me a much better slant for Svalbard and Longyearben. I adjusted the self-steering vane to bring the wind on the beam, eased out the mainsheet and reduced the sail to just two panels. After the usual final adjustments to get *M.* as perfectly balanced as possible on her new course, I ducked below and closed the hatch after me.

*Bloody hell!*

I had executed similar manoeuvres hundreds of times at sea, and the reward after working at the hatch, especially in cold and heavy weather, was the retreat to the haven of the cabin. There, I could stretch out on my bunk and doze happily to the sound of the water coursing along the hull, just a few inches from my ear. I could sit on my bunk and work at the chart table, whether plotting courses or positions, or writing up my logbooks. I prepared and ate my meals sitting on my bunk, the navigation space converted to a galley by simply swivelling the chart table aft. Sometimes I lay on my bunk with my head forward, so that I felt cocooned under the foredeck; usually I lay on my bunk with my head aft, enjoying the light flooding through the hatch. In good weather I could leave the hatch open and watch the clouds weaving around to the pitch and roll of the boat. The cabin was the perfect size – neither too big nor too small. Everything was to hand; everything had its allotted place; nothing was superfluous. It was the perfect manifestation of a minimalist mindset.

Everything had now been thrown out of kilter. There was nowhere for me to lie down and nowhere to sit, apart from the cabin sole and the companionway steps. I admit that for a fraction of a second I felt annoyed at this disruption of my carefully constructed realm, but I have trained myself to disarm annoyance as soon as I feel it bubbling up. It is an irrational and damaging emotion; to submit to it is a sign of weakness. Reminding myself that *the obstacle is the way*, I resolved to turn all the perceived difficulties into opportunities to learn and to experiment. *So you don't have your bunk anymore, sunshine? So what? What kind of layabout are you that needs a bunk?*

I knew that I would soon have to cook my evening meal, but first I needed some rest. I sat down on the cabin sole with my legs stretched out and my back against the companionway steps. It was the first moment of repose since spotting the liferaft just a couple of hours previously.

I began to make some rough calculations. If this wind held, we could be in the Isfjorden within four days or so. I had no permit to land in Svalbard but given the circumstances I doubted that there would be any trouble. In any case, I had no intention of staying. If I were to spend, say, two days at

Longyearben to deposit the girl and prepare for setting sail again, then in total I would lose about a week out of my cruising time. I ought to be able to construct a reasonable and satisfying voyage, despite this disruption. It would have a different trajectory from the one originally planned, as I doubted that I would want to retrace my track back to the north-west corner of the Greenland Sea, but there were other enticing possibilities to the north and east of Spitsbergen.

By now I was feeling much more positive. I could cope with this situation for four days, however uncomfortable it might be. It would be an interesting challenge, this sudden adaption to having two people on board.

I leaned forward so that my face was close to the sleeping Lárochka. I searched out her gloved hand under the covers and squeezed it gently.

*Ларочка… четыре дня… только четыре дня. Lárochka… four days… just four days.*

## 25

I prepared the pan of food standing by the stove, my head bent under the cabin roof, and ate it, straight from the pan as always, sitting on the cabin sole.

As I ate, I thought about Lárochka. She was still lying inert on my bunk, breathing but showing no sign of revival, despite the warm cocoon I had created for her. I had assumed that she was simply hypothermic, but now I wondered whether it was more complicated than that. From the little I knew about hypothermia, she would now either be dead, or would have revived somewhat as her body temperature rose. She seemed to be in suspension between those two states, in a kind of coma. Had the shock of what had happened induced some other medical problem? Or did she have some pre-existing condition? Diabetes? A heart weakness? There were scores of possibilities, and I had no way of diagnosing any of them and no way of treating any of them even if I knew what the problem was.

Worse still, it was impossible for me to get her to eat or drink in her comatose state. What if she were badly dehydrated? On an impulse I put the pan back on the stove and poured a small amount of water into my plastic drinking mug. Kneeling beside her, I lifted her head and put the mug to her lips. I had hoped that this might induce some reaction, that she might open her mouth wider, but nothing happened.

*Ларочка… пожалуйста… выпей немножко. Lárochka… please… drink a little.*

I tipped the mug enough for a few drops to run onto her lips. Again, there was no reaction. It was not worth continuing: there was a risk of choking her if I tried to pour liquid into her mouth. I drank the water in the mug myself, hung it on its hook and sat down again on the cabin sole with the rest of my meal to hand.

I was stymied. How do you make an unconscious person drink? Is it possible? I had no idea. In a hospital they could do it with drips and stomach tubes or whatever is the appropriate equipment. How long would she last without water? I seemed to recall that the limit was three or four days.

*Bloody hell!*

It would take me that long, at an absolute minimum, to get her ashore. The enormity of what was happening struck me fully for the first time. Thus far, I had only been concerned with getting the girl aboard and making her comfortable. I now realised that, if Lárochka did not revive soon, it may become a matter of life or death. And if she died, would I be responsible?

I pushed aside that question, along with all the other difficult questions that went along with it, and thought instead about what might have caused Lárochka to end up alone in a liferaft. I had the impression that she was a leisure sailor rather than a maritime professional; that she had been on a yacht rather than a ship. Her clothing and the small liferaft pointed to a sailing craft. I thought about the sail I had seen to the south of Jan Mayen. Was that the yacht? That was quite possible, given how few yachts sail these waters. Whichever vessel she was on, was she singlehanding or with a crew? And what caused the yacht to sink, assuming that this is what had happened? Had the yacht hit an ice floe and been holed? Had a whale collided with the yacht? My impression was that whatever happened had been sudden. There was nothing in the liferaft except the girl: no grab bag, no papers, no logbooks, no supplies of any kind. There had not been time to get properly organised. The liferaft had been thrown overboard, inflated and Lárochka had climbed into it, all in a matter of seconds. If she was not singlehanding, then the rest of the crew had not had time to save themselves.

And how long had she been in the liferaft before I found her? Given her state, I suspected that it was at least a day or two, possibly longer. That thought gave me another jolt. I had been calculating her three or four days of survival without water from when I found her, but to that I had to add the time before I found her. Maybe her time was already up.

*Jesus, what a mess!*

And what about Lárochka herself? Why was such a young woman sailing in such a remote place, whether singlehanded or on a crewed yacht? The only clue I had was her tattoo. She perhaps saw herself as an Arctic tern, as one of those wonderful bouncy, chatty birds that fly twelve thousand miles each year, the longest annual migration of any bird. She identified with that most free-spirited of ocean species, one of the most elegant and stream-lined, and for all its delicate structure, one of the hardiest. If that was the case, then she was a girl after my own heart. This was all no more than guesswork, based on the flimsiest of evidence, but if it were even partly true, then the girl was a kindred spirit.

I now felt strongly that she had been sailing on her own. That, of course, is what I wanted to believe, and for the moment I was free to believe anything I liked. It was helpful for me, in any event, to construct an identity for the girl. She was now more than moribund flesh taking up my bunk. She now had the makings of a personality, even if it were no more than a construct of my own imagination. I felt closer to her, and even more responsible for her. We shared the same fascination with the wild places. Were she conscious and talking, we could exchange ideas. Perhaps we could learn from each other; perhaps we could inspire each other. I felt a growing affection for Lárochka. She was clearly an exceptional young woman.

From my uncomfortable position on the cabin sole, my back against the companionway steps, I found her hand under the blankets and held it tight. Overcome by an onrush of exhaustion, I closed my eyes and fell asleep.

## 26

Even when I am sleeping, some part of my consciousness is always attuned to the motion of the ship, always alert to any change in the feel of the conditions. At some point later that evening I was woken by just such a change. For a second time, the wind had backed, this time to the south-west, and strengthened too, so that we were now pitching awkwardly in a south-easterly direction. I spent a couple of minutes in the hatchway, resetting the self-steering gear to bring the wind onto our starboard quarter, and reducing sail to just one panel. Even with that small footage of sail, we were now racing east with a following sea.

My spirits rose. We now had a perfect wind to get us quickly to the Isfjorden. Maybe we could be there in less than three days.

I closed the hatch and attended to Lárochka. The stove had

run out of fuel and stopped heating the cabin. I refilled the stove and relit it. The make-shift hot water bottles I had prepared for Lárochka had cooled right down. As I only had one pan, I scraped out the food left in it for the next day's breakfast into a spare bowl and filled the pan with the water from the two hot water bottles. It would be better to keep recycling that same water rather than using up fresh and precious drinking water each time.

While the water was heating, I settled down on the cabin sole with the ship's logbook and a pen, and brought it up to date as best I could. I normally note everything of relevance into the logbook as it happens, or very shortly afterwards. I had not had time to make a single entry since first sighting the liferaft, so I reconstructed what had happened retrospectively, guessing at the approximate times I had taken Lárochka aboard, made course and sail changes and so on.

Completing the ship's logbook helped to impose a sense of order and normality. I had cooked and eaten a meal, somehow managed to sleep for a while sitting on the cabin sole and was now up to date with the log. Maybe I could adapt to these changed circumstances after all.

I refilled the bottles with hot water and settled them in again on each side of Lárochka. She seemed unchanged. I knelt beside her on the cabin sole, found her hand under the covers and spoke to her in English.

*Lárochka…I am so glad I found you. What a terrible thought it is, that otherwise you would still be in that liferaft, drifting all alone on a cold, cold sea. I know that there is not much I can do for you except to make you warm and comfortable. I don't know whether that will be enough or not, but I'll do my best.*

As I whispered, my self-consciousness dissolved away.

*Lárochka…who are you, Lárochka? You are a stranger to me, but I feel I know you. Did I find you, or did you find me? Where have you come from? What is your story? Did you know that the Arctic tern is my favourite seabird? It's the bird that always makes me happy. So light. So effortless. So free. Lárochka…I would love to talk to you. I think we could be friends. I am an old man, yes, but we could be friends.*

I knew that I was rambling, with no order or sense to my words. Maybe the sense was not important. It was the act of talking, of making sound, of creating vibrations, that mattered. I may just as well sing or recite nonsense or make random noise. That thought gave me an idea. Scored indelibly into my memory were the closing lines of Pushkin's epic poem *Цыганы – The Gypsies*, learned by heart when I was a teenager. I began to recite them, my voice growing stronger as I progressed:

*Но счастья нет и между вами,*
*Природы бедные сыны!..*
*И под издранными шатрами*
*Живут мучительные сны,*
*И ваши сени кочевые*
*В пустынях не спаслись от бед,*
*И всюду страсти роковые,*
*И от судеб защиты нет.*

*

*Yet you, too, Nature's sons undaunted,*
*Are strangers to happiness, it seems!*
*Your ragged shelters, too, are haunted*

107

*By omens and oppressive dreams,*
*Deep in your wilderness, disaster*
*For wandering tents in ambush waits;*
*Grim passion everywhere is master,*
*And no one can elude the Fates.*

Yes, I recited these lines, without any forethought, and it was only after I had spoken them that I realised that these were not random sounds, but words with an awful relevance to that moment: even the gypsies roaming free on the wild steppes cannot escape the exigencies of fate.

# 27

I had spent many summers sailing in the High Arctic and had rarely been troubled by heavy weather The few storms I had experienced had been short-lived and relatively toothless. The benign high pressure system and twenty-four hour daylight of the high latitudes seem to take the sting out of any incipient bad weather. It is further south, where one encounters the depressions whisked eastwards by the jet stream, that the storms can ratchet themselves up into a genuinely threatening frenzy.

I had no doubt grown complacent about the possibility of extreme conditions so far north in summer, and I ought to have known better. To take the weather for granted when alone at sea does not perhaps qualify as a mortal sin, but it does suggest a severe lack of good judgement. To atone for that lapse, I can confess that as the south-westerly wind that was driving us on so quickly towards Spitsbergen began to gust more strongly, I was not in the least concerned. I doubted that the increasing wind would last very long, or that it would reach true gale force or beyond. There would be some short-lived discomfort before a return to the soft-edged Arctic weather I knew so well.

Adjustments needed to be made, nonetheless. We were racing too quickly, and risked broaching should a hard gust catch us at the wrong moment. I reduced sail to just half a panel and altered our course so that we were running a little more off the wind. Our heading was now somewhat north of east, but this did not concern me, as I viewed it as no more than a temporary measure; we could resume our easterly heading once this wind blew itself out.

The increasingly boisterous motion, particularly our more pronounced rolling as we ran downwind, was creating difficulties as regards Lárochka. I could keep her body steady by means of the bunk straps, but each time we rolled her head was whisked alarmingly from one side to the other. Whatever pillows or supports I used to restrict the movement of her head refused to stay in place for more than a minute or two. To solve the problem, I sat down on the cabin sole, facing aft, and used my left hand to hold on to her shapka and stop her head from rolling around. As a precaution, I also turned off the stove; I did not want the flame burning while there was a risk that a violent roll could force fuel out of its reservoir.

I think back now and am embarrassed for all the complacent delusions I was happy to entertain throughout that first night with Lárochka aboard. Sitting on the cabin sole in a supremely uncomfortable position, my left arm stretched out and holding her head steady, my fatigued mind wandering idly, I began to picture myself as some sort of hero. I was effecting a Great Rescue. Once I had delivered the girl to Longyearben, it would become a big story. SOLO SAILOR SAVES RUSSIAN GIRL IN ARCTIC. There would be newspaper interviews, maybe television appearances too. I would of course be modest. *It was nothing, really. Any sailor would have done it.* I would be able to write a book about it. My Russian publisher would snap it up, too. Maybe the Russians would give me a medal. And once Lárochka had recovered, I would get to know her properly. Her gratitude for me saving her would be limitless. Yes, all this discomfort, the abandonment of my original plans, the stress and worry, will more than reap their rewards. Hell, once this is all over, I'll become a legend!

Thus lulled by premature, prideful nonsense, I dozed on and off. The wind blew hard and on we ran, racing innocently into the fickle arms of destiny.

*

The weakly-lit night turned to a weakly-lit day and the wind still blew. I was stiff and aching from an uncomfortable night spent bracing myself on the cabin sole. I was cold too. I had given Lárochka all but one of my coverings, a pink woollen blanket - made by McCallum and Craigie Ltd, of Glasgow, Scotland, By Appointment To H.M. Queen Elizabeth II Blanket Manufacturers - that had belonged to my Scottish grandmother. I had wrapped it around me as best I could and shivered until breakfast-time. The blanket may have been just the ticket for a summer's night in Balmoral, but the Greenland Sea soon showed up its limitations.

A fair old sea had built up throughout the night and it was too dangerous to light the stove. I ate my breakfast cold out of the bowl I had scraped it into and washed it down with a couple of swigs from my water bottle.

Fool that I was, I thought that the wind would soon ease, and that we would be able to resume our heading straight for the Isfjorden. I had several times sailed past that mighty fjord's wide mouth, a few miles offshore, and was glad to have a legitimate excuse to sail up to Longyearben, Svalbard's main settlement. The administrative hoops for obtaining permission to land on Svalbard include posting a sizeable financial bond and having a current firearms licence, so I could by-pass all that nonsense with impunity.

Lárochka seemed unchanged. I could just make out the movement of her breathing. Occasionally her lower lip quivered for a second or two. Her body was still alive but what about her mind? Is a coma nothing but blackness, an empty, meaningless hole, or is it filled with dreams and images, like sleep? Was her mind still working at some sub-conscious level? Could she hear my voice when I spoke to her? Could she understand the words, or if not the words, the meaning conveyed by the tone of the sounds? She had opened her eyes just once, when I had first found her, revealing her startling blue irises. Had she registered anything during that moment? Her eyes had not seemed to focus on my face. I suspected that she had no idea, even in the deepest recesses of her mind, of what was happening, but I could not be sure. I suspected, again with no way of knowing whether I was right or wrong, that if I talked to her there was more chance of her finding her way out of whatever mental prison she was trapped in, than if

I kept silent. I had several times held her hand, instinctively, and I realised she might be as responsive to touch as much as to sound. Both are no more than activations of the nervous system, via different mechanisms. I resolved to be less shy about touching her.

I know, I know – this is the sort of thing that anybody with experience of the sick and the dying is perfectly aware of, but I had not had that experience. I had no choice but to think about it and work out what I should do from first principles. I had to overcome prejudices and embarrassments and open myself up to a new and alien set of behaviours. It was hard – an old man cannot turn himself into Florence Nightingale overnight.

I decided that I would spend more time talking to Lárochka, that I would hold and squeeze her hand and not be embarrassed about caressing her cheek or patting her thigh. I realise now that this was a way for me to overcome my sense of helplessness. I had no idea what was wrong with her and no way of treating her and so was condemned to the role of a mere observer, a passive, useless onlooker. I needed something positive to grasp on to, however insubstantial it may be. The only therapy that I had to give to Lárochka was my voice and my physical presence. If, somewhere deep down, she could hear me and feel my touch, and if, by some small chance, that would help her, then it was my duty to do what I could.

# 28

As far as I can recall, it was only a few hours after eating my cold breakfast that I was forced to lower the remaining panel of the sail, lash the sail bundle to its gallows and run before the wind, at just a slight angle to it. Our heading was now almost north-east.

I had assumed that the wind would soon ease, but I was wrong: it seemed to be winding itself up into a full gale. I wondered whether it was our relative proximity to the Greenland icecap that was the cause of this fury. When I had sailed to the Davis Strait, to the west of Greenland, I had been careful to keep well to the south of Greenland's southern tip, Cape Farvel, an area well known for its violent storms. Maybe this unpredictable weather was a more general phenomenon around Greenland. Maybe, too, the interplay of the warm Gulf Stream and the cold East Greenland Current created unusual atmospheric conditions.

I knelt on the cabin sole, leaning over Lárochka and holding her head between my palms.

*Well, Lárochka, it's getting a bit wild out there. Can you hear that wind? It's shrieking a bit in the gusts now. It's a bloody cold wind too. We'll be OK. We're under bare poles now and we can run on quite happily. Have you been in many storms? I've been in loads and they're not much fun. This one won't last, though. They never do round here in the summer. It's hardly a storm anyway, just the odd gust at gale force. It should ease off soon. I'm sorry it's cooler in here than I'd like, but I daren't light the stove. I can't do your hot water bottles either. I'm sorry about that, but you should be warm enough. I bet where you come from, you're used to the cold. I have a friend from Siberia, and she says it gets to minus forty there in the winter. Or maybe you're from the north, from the White Sea or somewhere like that. That's just as bad in winter. You're a strong, tough girl. Just hang in there, Lárochka. I'm counting on you to hang in there. Just another day or two and we'll get you sorted out.*

I spoke in English and as I rambled on, searching for the sounds that might give Lárochka some comfort, my shyness eased. I had never had company in heavy weather. It was a novel experience to be able to dissipate, through words, the tension that always comes with threatening conditions.

*Lárochka, I'm so glad you're here. So glad I found you. Honestly. I was a bit worried at first, you know. There's not much room in here and I'm still not sure how I'm going to sleep properly, but never mind. I'm honoured to have you as a passenger. It's amazing to have you here, so unexpectedly. It's not something I could ever have imagined. I still have no idea where you came from but what the hell! You're here now, on my little ship. And Lárochka, I was going to say, about the Arctic tern. I'm so glad that you chose it for your tattoo. I adore those birds. What a coincidence that you must like them too. One day we'll talk about why you chose it. And I need freedom too. That's why I make these voyages, to be totally free to roam wherever I like. And listen. Can you hear that wind still getting up? I'd better give everything a quick check. I'll be back.*

I opened the hatch, and with my head protected by the folding canvas hood, surveyed the scene. It was far from the biggest sea I had ever seen, but it was starting to look nasty, with breaking crests rolling forward and wave faces streaked with foam. As ever, fulmars wheeled around us or sat in bobbing, tightly packed groups, not in the least troubled by the developing maelstrom. I envied them their ease, but after all this was their home, not mine. I was the interloper, the provisional, awkward trespasser, pushing possibility to the limit with my little boat and my little sail, and almost literally out of my depth. I remembered a well-worn homily: *Life begins at the end of your comfort zone.* Well, if that was the case, I was about to really start living.

＊

I closed the hatch and returned to my vigil beside Lárochka. It is always surprising how peaceful the cabin of a tiny yacht can feel when a storm is raging outside. We were taking the odd blow as the crest of a breaking wave hissed past, thudding into the quarter and lurching us to leeward. I locked the after portlight, so that the cabin was now completely sealed. I always rebuild my yachts to make them totally watertight and unsinkable, and have many times felt the benefit of this: it provides an element of reassurance when conditions become worrying.

In fact, I was not especially concerned at that point. *M.* had handled seas like this many times before. There were just two aspects of the situation that were gnawing at me. The first was that our speed had been reduced considerably. We were probably making about a knot and a half of downwind drift at most, much less than our progress before I had been forced to take off all sail. The longer this lasted, the less the chance of getting Lárochka to Longyearben in good time. We were being pushed to the north-east too, and this was starting to raise questions in my mind. Somewhere to the north of us was the edge of the pack-ice. It was now almost a month since we had set sail, and I had no idea how the ice had moved during that period. It ought to have receded, but by how much? The more we were forced northwards, the greater the risk of encountering sea-ice of some sort. Meeting ice of any density under these conditions would be like being driven onto a merciless lee shore. There would be no way to escape. It would not be survivable.

*Lárochka…can you hear me? I hope so. It's still a bit wild out there, but it can't last much longer. We'll get you to Longyearben, don't worry. This is just a bit of a hold-up. Once it eases, we'll pile on plenty of sail, I promise. Ha! We'll have you there in no time, you'll see. Then you can get properly sorted out. But please hang in there, Lárochka. Please. You can do it, I know. You're young and strong. You can hang on for a day or two. I know you can. I'm counting on you, Lárochka. Think of your mum and dad. Maybe you've got brothers and sisters too, maybe a boyfriend. Hang in there for them too, not just for me. Lárochka, you're young and strong and beautiful. You can do it. Think of the Arctic terns. Twelve thousand miles of flying every single year! What strength! What commitment! What beauty! You're just as tough as an Arctic tern. I'm sure of that. Keep going, Lárochka. Please, please, keep going.*

# 29

As I write this story, I keep track of the word-count. So far, on the first draft anyway, I have written 29,903 words. That includes a few notes I have written for the ending, and the quotation, from the eleventh century Persian poet Omar Khayām, that I have already chosen to preface the work, should I complete it.

It has taken thirty thousand hard-mined words, then, to bring us to the start of the real story. Everything so far has been a prelude to the main theme. When I started writing, I had no idea whether I would be able to write a hundred words or a hundred thousand words. Or whether I would be able to write anything at all. It is perhaps only the discipline acquired over many years of authorship that has enabled me not just to start this task, but to keep going right to the heart of the matter. I have simply plugged away at my minimum five hundred words per day, every single day, word after word, sentence after sentence, chapter after chapter, without too much depth of thought, fuelled by a blind faith that if I just *keep going*, I might somehow manage to tell the tale.

I have forced myself to start writing, every single morning, fearful that if I pause the effort, I may lose my momentum and abandon the project. It would be so easy to give up, especially now that the hard kernel of the story is almost upon us. Were I to abandon my task, nobody would ever know that I lacked the strength or the courage to carry on. It would remain my secret, along with the secrets of the voyage I am recounting. The world will not stop in its tracks for not knowing what happened that summer. It is so tempting to take the easy route out, to keep to the deep, wide offshore waters and so avoid the shoals and rocks amongst which the telling of this story might land me.

Yes, it is tempting to abandon the words I have so far written, to force myself once more to forget, to revert to the convenient amnesia which has carried me through the last few years. Despite that temptation, I know that I must *keep going*. I must purge myself of the burden I have been carrying, otherwise I will never be at peace.

I must remember, too, that this expurgation is not just about me and my own petty state of mind. This is not only my story, it is Lárochka's too. I must write it for her as much as for myself. She deserves better than an eternal silence. For her sake, as well as my own, I must *keep going*. I had almost managed to forget about her, in a wilful act of exclusion from my memory. Now that I am recreating our time together, trying as best I can to relive every moment, the better to communicate it, I realise what an unforgivable injustice that deliberate forgetting has been. I feel deeply ashamed for having excised her from my thoughts for so long. I made a promise that I would keep her in the forefront of my mind, but I allowed that promise to lapse. For many years I have deluded myself, lied to myself, by means of a disgraceful sin of omission. To stop writing now would add yet another injury to the injustices I have already meted out to her.

*Lárochka…please forgive me. I am telling our tale, at last. It has taken a long time to reach this point, I know, and you deserve so much better. I'm not in the least proud of myself, and having stripped myself bare, I'm starting to see myself with fresh eyes. It may be too late to make amends. I do not deserve absolution by means of a simple confession; that ecclesiastical expedient has always struck me as too easy. I need to suffer, and maybe my guilt will power that suffering. Lárochka…now that I am writing our story, I think about you every day. You have once again become a looming presence in my waking hours. How could I have forgotten about you so easily? How could I have abandoned you so carelessly? How could I have been so cruel? Are all our lives composed of endless acts of casual malevolence that pass by unnoticed? We have so little time and so little inclination to reexamine every action. Lárochka…I will make amends, I promise. I neither expect nor deserve forgiveness for my long silence, but I will carry on with my task. I will see our story through to its end, that I promise. It is the least I can do.*

# 30

We were under bare poles, then, running easily, for a while anyway, to the north-east. It was by no means an ideal situation, but at sea things can always be worse than they are, and I was not unduly worried. The belief that conditions would soon ease had not yet evaporated; it was just a matter of time and patience.

I no longer dared to light the stove and so I ate my food cold in a cooling cabin. With the cabin sealed and two of us inside, the temperature was tolerable for me, perhaps about five degrees Celsius, but no doubt inadequate for Lárochka. I added a spare snowboarding jacket to her pile of coverings and leaned over her from my kneeling position on the cabin sole, my right shoulder and arm across her body, trying to transmit as much warmth as I could.

Perhaps twelve or fifteen hours passed in this way before an abrupt change. Within a matter of minutes, the wind backed a couple of points and ratcheted itself up to a severe gale, a fully-fledged Force 9.

*Bloody hell!*

This was not at all what I had been expecting. Not only were we now in a sea state that was building dangerously, our heading had also changed to north-north-east or thereabouts, taking us further away from Longyearben and more directly towards the ice.

That was the moment when I realised that I had been deluding myself about the impossibility of seriously heavy weather, here, at this time of year. I could feel the intent in the wind thudding into us as we crested every wave; I could hear the lack of compromise in the pitch of its screaming through the running rigging. At that moment I knew in my head and in my heart that, summer or not, we were in for a real Arctic storm; that it was not going to be short-lived; that things were going to get much, much worse.

*Bloody hell!*

I had to prepare for storm conditions with a comatose, half-dead passenger on board. A severe gale is bad enough under normal circumstances. How the hell was I going to manage? How was I going to keep Lárochka warm and secure once things really livened up?

For a minute or two I abandoned Lárochka and studied the sea through the after portlight. Its surface was a confusion of foamy streaks under a haze of spray whipped off the wavetops by the wind. Those wavetops were reaching higher and rolling forward more aggressively as the sea built. The chances of being caught side on by one of those breaking crests and put on our beam ends were increasing inexorably.

I would soon have to make a crucial decision. Do I launch my Jordan series drogue now or hang on for a little while in the hope that conditions might ease? The drogue is made up of almost a hundred metres of heavy line onto which are threaded 86 miniature sea anchors, small strong cones, which act as brakes if the boat is thrown forward. At the after end of the line there is chain and an anchor, to weigh the line down and make sure the cones are always well below the surface of the waves.

The drogue is my last resort in life-threatening conditions, but the decision whether to launch it or not is always finely balanced. It was a big commitment to deploy it. I would have to spend time on deck in a very exposed position making all the necessary preparations. I had been through this procedure twice before, once off south-west Iceland and once to the south-east of Greenland and knew that it was not to be taken lightly. Once launched and operational, the drogue would certainly defuse any threat from a dangerous following sea, but it was difficult to retrieve in rough conditions, using little more than the strength of my arms. To deploy the drogue prematurely and to no purpose would be a huge waste of energy; to deploy it too late might lead to a capsize or worse.

I watched the sea, trying to judge its mood and debating the pros and cons of setting the drogue. The thought of having to exit the hatch and spend time in the cockpit and on the tiny afterdeck, quite possibly with waves washing over me as I worked to prepare everything, was enough to argue against the idea. I also thought about Lárochka. The drogue defuses the following sea, but it also changes the motion of the yacht. For some reason it encourages a much more exaggerated roll to each side. I had always found it impossible to stay in my bunk, even when lashed in, with such a violent roll, and had always taken to the cabin sole when the drogue was set. There, with the lower centre of gravity, and with the bunk sides and locker sides restricting how far one can be thrown, it was much more comfortable. What the hell would I do with Lárochka if I set the drogue? It would be murderous for her on the bunk. For the moment, I had no idea.

I watched the sea and listened to the wind and rehearsed the sequence of actions necessary for launching the drogue. It was necessary to do things quickly and efficiently and in the right order. Any mistake could be costly. I had still not made up my mind, but I pulled on my wet weather gear regardless. I had to be ready to act without any delay.

Yes, I watched the sea and listened to the wind and steeled myself for the prospect of exiting the hatch. The more I watched and listened, the more inevitable that sortie on deck became. I was already fatigued from lack of sleep and from the stresses of the previous day or two. I did not feel at all strong, either physically or mentally. I really did not want to do it, but I could sense that the wind was gusting even more ferociously and that the waves were piling up even more steeply. I knelt beside Lárochka.

*Lárochka…I'm going to have to leave you for a while. I don't think I have a choice now. It's getting pretty bad out there and I've got to launch the drogue. We'll be much safer once it's deployed. I'll be as quick as I can, but it will take me a while. I don't want to leave you all alone down here, but I really have to go on deck. It'll be for the best in the long run. I'll make you as comfortable as I can before I go. Remember that you're not alone. I won't be far away.*

*And once this storm's over we'll get you to Longyearben as quick as we can. So hang in there. Keep going, Lárochka, keep going.*

I rearranged the pillows and bags around her head, slipped on and buckled my harness and opened the hatch. I leaned out over the bridge deck and clipped my two harness tethers to the appropriate U-bolts set in the deck. Then it was up and out into the fury unleashed.

How does one even start to describe this kind of scene to a landsman who has never known it? The limited palette of descriptive words available to the writer have long since become clichés, long since lost their power. In any case, it is not the individual components - the wind, the waves, the driving spray, the roaring sea and so on - that define such a demented seascape. The whole is much, much greater than the sum of its parts. All the elements that make up the scene fuse together, multiplying their individual force a thousand times as they merge into one overpowering unity. It is Nature in all its magnificence and in all its horror; physics at the limit of what it can create from the interacting energies and pressures of the planet. It is a reminder of the power of the universe and the utter insignificance of all the little creatures that cling on to their little rock and their little lives.

I climbed out of the hatch, dropped down into the cockpit and closed the hatch after me. For a moment I was mesmerised by the uncompromising violence that stretched in every direction to the hazy horizons. I realised that I had underestimated the strength of the wind. It was now a good Force 10. The surface of the sea was scarcely visible under the layer of foam and spray scoured off the waves and driven downwind in an almost solid, stinging mass.

Yes, for a moment I stood there, my head empty of thought, overawed by the stupendous brutality of the forces at work. It was a fury beyond rational analysis. For a second or two I let it wash over me, giving myself up to the moment, allowing my fear to dissipate, feeling the most exquisitely intense *aliveness*.

Ha! This *aliveness* may not last long! I realised that I had left things later than I should have. I was going to have to disconnect the self-steering lines, and for the several minutes between the disconnection of those lines and the deployment of the drogue, we would be drifting out of control and, inevitably, beam on to the breaking seas. I yanked the five lines that control the self-steering gear out of their cam cleats, bunched them together, coiled them and dropped them on the after deck. Next task was to disconnect the steering chain from the tiller and anchor the tiller amidships with bungee cords. We were now drifting free, with the worst part of the job still to come. I had to climb onto the after deck and rotate the self-steering pendulum out of the water, then lash it upright alongside the wind vane. I moved slowly aft, shifting the anchor points of my tethers one by one. It was something of a fairground ride on that tiny after deck as we pitched and rolled and dropped twenty feet or so into each trough. I was on my knees, straining to get the pendulum clear of the water. Once it had broken free of the surface it swung easily into its upright position and I quickly lashed it in place with the line always kept there for that purpose.

Then it was back to the cockpit, transferring the tether points as I went. As I said earlier, the drogue itself is stored in bins on each side of the cockpit. I unhooked the canvas covers of the bins and found the inboard end of the drogue. This had to be attached to the drogue bridle…and so on and so on.

I'm not going to go through every single part of the process of deploying the drogue. This book is not conceived as a manual of seamanship and the technical minutiae are of little relevance to the story. Suffice to say that the preparations required a series of tasks, best done in a pre-determined, methodical order. We were rolled heavily several times during the process and as far as I can recall, just one wave came aboard and filled the small cockpit while I was standing in it.

Once the drogue was securely attached to the bridle, the long loop of rope anchored with strong chainplates to each quarter of the boat, and once the bridle itself had been passed over the top of the self-steering gear, I was ready to start feeding out the drogue. This is done from the inboard end, so that at first the drogue forms a loop in the water. That loop grows in length as the drogue is fed out hand over hand from the bins. Once the anchor and chain at the end of the drogue line is reached, they are thrown overboard and within half a minute or so, as the drogue extends to its full length and settles properly beneath the surface, the yacht is brought back stern on to the waves and the drogue starts to work its magic.

For a minute or two I sat on the bridge deck just aft of the cabin and checked that everything was in order and working properly. Facing aft, into the wind, my face was red-raw and stinging from the ice-cold spray driven on by the gale and my vision badly distorted by the sea water on the lenses of my glasses. I could already start to feel the elastic push and pull of the drogue and the strange way it seems to calm a following sea.

I remembered the long winter's evenings spent attaching the cones to the drogue line – a slow, repetitive job done in comfort in front of a glowing fire. Everything then had been theoretical, based on objective premises, a series of 'what-ifs'. Here now was the reality, that same line and those same cones shifted from the warmth of an Essex living room to ply their trade in an Arctic wilderness. I felt a kind of complicity with that line and those cones. I had assembled everything with my own hands, threaded every tape and tied every single knot (six for each cone, and therefore five hundred and sixteen tapes to be threaded through the line and five hundred and sixteen knots to anchor them). I too had been shifted from that warm Essex living room to ply my trade in an Arctic wilderness. I had created that drogue and now, I knew for sure, I was dependent on it for my survival.

*Jesus!*

I had been so absorbed in my work, so transfixed by the glorious insanity of the seascape, that I had forgotten about Lárochka. She too depended on the drogue for her survival. And on me, too.

*Jesus! What a mess!*

There was nothing more to be done on deck. I opened the hatch and, timing the moment to avoid any sudden lurches, half stood up and transferred my feet to the top step of the companionway, climbed down the steps, unhooked my tethers and closed the hatch firmly after me.

# 31

The deed was done. All control of the yacht had been ceded to the drogue. As far as the management of *M.* was concerned, I was now redundant. I had become little more than a passenger, a supernumerary, a passive onlooker rather than an active participant. In some ways it was a relief. I was exhausted to the core from the pressure of making decisions and from the endless activity flowing from them. It was a transition from activist to fatalist. I had done all I could do and now I was able, in a strange way, to relax and give myself up to whatever might happen.

Luckily the dousing from the wave which had come aboard had not penetrated my waterproofs and sea boots, but I still brought liberal amounts of seawater into the cabin. I rubbed my waterproofs with a towel and mopped up the drips on the cabin sole. In storm conditions I always keep my wet weather gear on, in case I have to exit the hatch quickly, but I like to keep the cabin as dry as possible.

I knelt beside Lárochka and held her head steady between my hands. She was pale, lifeless save for her irregular, shallow breaths. She was oblivious of the storm, oblivious of the danger, oblivious, it seemed, of me. I wondered whether that may be the ideal state. Oblivion.

*Well, Lárochka, it's done. I've launched the drogue. There's nothing more I can do now. We'll just have to ride it out and hope for the best. You're going to be too uncomfortable on this bunk, what with all the rolling. I think I'll have to make up something warm and soft for both of us on the cabin sole. There's nowhere else, really. Anyway, I won't be going on deck again, or I hope not. I won't leave you again. Thank you for being here, Lárochka. I've never had company in a storm before. Ha! You're not the most talkative, but I appreciate your being here. Really. And I know I keep saying it, but do keep going. It could be a while before we get to Longyearben. This blow is messing up my plans. But never mind. Just keep going. Держись крепко, Ларочка! Hold strong, Lárochka!*

\*

In all the years since that voyage, I have never tried to track the evolution of the weather system we found ourselves in. As an Arctic sailor, I ought to have had at least some curiosity as to how such a depression could have infiltrated the northern summer. I have always considered it to be an anomaly, but maybe, if I were to look more closely at the meteorological records, I would find that it was not so unusual after all.

Perhaps I had been lulled into complacency by the series of benign summers I had spent up there.

In any case, I have felt no desire whatsoever to study the weather charts for that summer. The memories are too raw; the whirl of closely spaced isobars I would no doubt find on the maps would remind of too many things I would like to forget. Even now, as I do my best to recreate what happened, I have no inclination to do any objective research on the matter. The story is too deeply personal to turn into a half-baked doctoral thesis. I don't know how this storm developed, and I have no wish to know. Does the man struck by lightning show much subsequent interest in the electrical properties of thunderstorms? Is the passenger of a derailed train concerned about the finer points of tracklaying? In most cases, the cause is secondary to the result.

*

I worked quickly, using my clothes' bags to create a makeshift mattress on the cabin sole. I also made sure I had plenty of easily consumed food to hand: energy bars, some apples, some pieces of fruitcake.

*Bloody hell!*

I had an urgent need to empty my bowels. Well, it was going to happen sooner or later. I would just have to get on with it. I opened the hatch, leaned out and using its line, pulled my toilet bucket out of the cockpit. Normally I have to dip it over the side to get some water into it, but with the waves that that had been climbing aboard it was already full. I emptied it until there was just a couple of inches in the bottom and brought it down into the cabin, closing the hatch after me. With my feet I shifted some of the bags I had put on the cabin sole, to create a space for the bucket. That was followed by my usual ritual of tearing a couple of sheets of kitchen roll into quarters.

*I'm sorry about this, Lárochka. I've no choice. Better to do it now, anyway, before we get settled down.*

I did my business as quickly as I could, opened the hatch and flung the contents of the bucket over the side. Usually, I scrubbed the bucket before dropping it back into the cockpit, but that nicety seemed redundant: it was more important to get the hatch closed and the cabin sealed as quickly as possible. I cleaned my hands with hand gel and wiped my face with a towel.

*Well, we're kind of quits now, Lárochka.*

I set up the temporary mattress again and untied Lárochka's bunk straps. I stripped off all her coverings, pushing them to the aft end of the bunk, and took a firm hold of her under her shoulders, with my left arm, and manoeuvred her torso round and off the bunk. I braced my feet as firmly as I could against each side of the cabin sole, hoping there would not be a nasty roll as I transferred her to her new bed. I grabbed her under the knees with my right arm and in one movement swung her round and squatted down as low as I could go, before letting her slide down onto the clothes bags. There was not enough length on the cabin sole for her to stretch out completely, so I folded her legs under her knees and let them fall to one side.

The final manoeuvre was to insert myself between Lárochka and the companionway steps. I lifted her torso and sat down behind her, my back against the ladder. My legs were each side of her, with her back against my stomach and her head on my chest. I pulled the coverings off the aft end of the bunk and arranged them over the both of us as well as I could, tucking them under my thighs.

*Well, there we are, Lárochka. It's the best I can do. I hope you're comfortable.*

I put my arms around her, to hold her as still as possible and to warm her up as best I could, then settled myself in for the calvary ahead.

*

Storms. I have lived through many of them in my little cockleshells and I thought I knew what the word signified. I was soon to learn that I had only a half-formed conception of the realities of extreme weather. Yes, it would soon become clear that everything I had so far tasted in the way of gales and severe gales and rough seas was nothing but an hors-d'oeuvre to the dish that was about to be served up, no more than a titillating appetizer. My palate was about to be brutally re-educated.

With nothing to do now except to hold on tightly to Lárochka, I could close my eyes and give all my senses over to the sound of the wind and waves and the strange motion induced by the series drogue.

The wind was now shrieking in a cacophony of conflicting pitches. Every protuberance above the deck was vibrating and howling at its own resonance as the air and spray tore past. I would gladly have closed off my ears to this chorus of demented ghouls, but the sound was too deep-seated to escape: the mast and the hull and anything with the least flexibility had become a vast sounding-board, magnifying the vibrations. Every bone in my body seemed to be quivering at the frequencies soaked up from the cabin sole and the steps against which I was leaning. I had been absorbed physically into the texture of the storm. There was no escaping it as I was now part of it, no more than another form of matter subject to the laws of physics, every cell of my body acted upon by the transfer of energy from the maelstrom outside.

The gusts came in more strongly and more regularly, ratcheting up the vibrations until they became a palpable shaking. The thirty feet of unstayed mast above the deck were convulsing in each onslaught, sending paroxysms of movement through the mast partners to the coach roof, and through the mast step to the hull itself. This universal shaking was compounded by the rat-tat-tatting of the main halyard against the mast, an ugly, insistent, inescapable, unbearable tattoo that presages nothing good and which over time can drive a man crazy.

The only saving grace in the situation was that the series drogue had largely disarmed the ferocity of the sea. Moving slowly downwind with the stern always squared off to the movement of the waves, we were no longer taking blows on the quarter or on the beam. The occasional breaking crest rushed past us with a hiss, but the drogue regulated our speed to the force of each wave, neutralising the threat of a serious pooping. The drogue creates an extraordinarily supple movement, reminiscent of a kind of horizontal bungee rope. As the wave pushes it forward, the boat is smoothly decelerated by the drogue and lifted almost to a point of weightlessness before being settled gently down on the after slope of the wave and the following trough. With Lárochka in my arms, we were subjected to this endless push and pull, with its accompanying elastic rise and fall, for hour after hour. The soft, almost soporific flow of this motion was all at odds with the hard-edged whine and clatter of the wind.

*Well, Lárochka, what d'you think of all this?*

Her ear was just a few inches from my lips.

*It ain't much fun, is it? God knows how long this is going to last. I hope you're warm enough there, and comfy. Not much else I can do, I'm afraid.*

I was glad that I was not alone, glad that I had someone to hold on to. I clasped Lárochka tightly to my chest and nestled my nose into the fur of her shapka.

# 32

How many hours passed like that? I have no idea. Maybe five or six. Perhaps ten or twelve. Maybe more. Adrift in a hellish storm on a hellish sea, we had moved outside the compass of normal, reasonable human existence and moved, too, outside of any meaningful concept of time. Minutes became hours; hours passed like minutes. I occasionally dozed, lulled by the motion and the roaring wind, but on waking had no idea whether I had slept for seconds or for hours. I had stopped looking at my watch. There was no point. Time had been of the absolute essence as far as getting Lárochka to Longyearben was concerned, but something more powerful had eclipsed the merely temporal. Longyearben might now just as well be a million miles away, or a trillion. We might be there in a week, or a month, or a century. We had been swept up into a node of such elemental force that the future, or any thoughts about the future, had lost all substance. There was nothing but the now, nothing but an all-consuming actuality.

Some hazy, sub-conscious corner of my brain was still trying to process, through habit, the meteorology of what was happening. I had a vague expectation that things would soon ease and that the wind would veer to the west or north-west, bringing us back to a more acceptable heading.

*Ha! Dream on, sunshine! You wouldn't know a weather system if it hit you straight in the kisser!*

Yes, yet again I had both underestimated and misinterpreted what was happening. I had thought that the wind had reached the limit of what was possible, but I was wrong. At some point in my semi-comatose state, I realised that the pitch of the shrieking had risen by a tone or two and that the vibrations pulsing through hull and decks had become even more persistent and industrial.

*Bloody hell!*

Even worse, a glance at my reciprocal compass showed that our heading was shifting further to the north.

*Jesus!*

My imprecations were by now tired, resigned. The wind seemed to be backing further, contrary to my expectations, and sending us even more directly towards the pack-ice. The wind-shift also explained the increase in the violence of our rolling and the feeling I had that the drogue was less settled to its task. We were now in a somewhat more confused cross-sea and the occasional errant wavetop thudded into us at an angle.

For the first time, a cloud of doubt passed through my mind. For the first time, I entertained the notion that this storm might not be survivable. The forces now acting on us were way beyond anything I had ever experienced, and I began to wonder whether my lightly built yacht would be able to resist them for much longer. And even if *M.* did hold together, and even if the drogue continued to do its work, there was now an increasingly strong chance that we would be driven into the ice to the north of us.

*It's not looking too good, Lárochka. I wish I could say otherwise. God knows what's going to happen. This wind's still getting stronger. And it's backed even more, which is the worst thing that could have happened. I think we're still a fair way from the ice, but to be honest I have no idea. For all I know there may be patches of stray sea ice anywhere ahead of us. That doesn't bear thinking about. I don't have a liferaft. The boat is unsinkable – but ice, that's another matter. I'm sorry about this, Lárochka. I so wanted to get you to Longyearben quickly. You're so young. It's so unfair. I'm an old man. A very lucky old man, really, considering all the things I've been through. I'd tell you about all the times I've nearly drowned at sea, but maybe now is not the time. Anyway, the point is that if we don't survive, it doesn't matter too much for me. I should have died many times over and somehow I didn't. I've had a long life and a good life. I can't complain. But you, Lárochka. So young, with everything ahead of you. An Arctic tern, too! I really would like to think that we have a few things in common, Lárochka. The thought gives me such pleasure. but I might just be kidding myself. We do tend to believe what we want to believe. If we don't survive, I'll never know one way or the other, so I may as well believe it. There's nothing to lose. I wonder if you've read any of the Russian editions of my books. I hope so. Maybe you know more about me than I know about you! There are so many things I want to know, Lárochka. So many questions. So many things to talk about.*

I hugged her unmoving and unresponsive body as tightly as I could and dozed on and off to the diabolic lullaby of an Arctic tempest.

*

I think that it was sometime after the wind shifted almost to the south that the accumulated tensions and lack of rest of the previous two or three days began to affect me. In a half-sitting position on the cabin sole, with the hard wood of the companionway steps pressing into my back, proper sleep was almost impossible. I was reaching a point of exhaustion, with no respite in prospect. This was the kind of situation I had always tried to avoid; a tired mind makes poor decisions. I had always made sure, as best I could, that I was well rested and therefore capable of sound judgement. I had been caught up in this whirlwind of unforeseen events and rushed along from one thing to another with no time to rest properly. My body was sore and stiff from several days spent on the cabin sole. Worse still, I could sense that my mind, drained to its limit from tiredness and tension, was starting to wander. I have many times escaped the oppressive, debilitating effects of heavy weather at sea through deep sleep, but this now seemed impossible. The drogue was set and there was nothing more I could do as far as the management of the ship was concerned, but my position on the cabin sole was so uncomfortable that I could only nap in short spells, and even then, I was never sure whether I had in fact slept. There seemed to be less and less distinction between my waking and my sleeping states; they were merging one into the other to form a disjointed but continuous nightmare. The screeching of the wind was inescapable, as was the constant juddering of the mast. My legs were braced to hold both Lárochka and myself steady against the violent rolling. If I relaxed them, we were both flung one way or the other into the bunk and locker sides.

*

Yes, I had reached the limit of what seemed bearable, but the human mind is infinitely resourceful. At that point a strange thing happened: I passed through a kind of doorway into that state of grace that comes with complete acceptance. This is not to say that I began to enjoy the torture of the moment, but that it slowly faded to the background as my mind wandered further from the physical and the actual, drifting away into another, less substantial state. I can see now that this was no more than an inbuilt mechanism for coping with the extremes of the moment, an escape from reality through the play of the imagination.

As every hour passed and my fatigue grew, I became less and less connected with the material world that was assaulting us so comprehensively. I found refuge in fragments of memory, in jumbled mental images, and in words. I talked to Lárochka, but whether it was aloud or simply in my mind, I have no idea. All I can remember is that as I clutched on to her, I found I had more and more to say. She had become a symbol: she was no longer just Lárochka, but all the women I have known. I held her in my arms and in so doing embraced once again all the loves of my life.

Perhaps, by then, I had given up hope of survival. I don't

know. An imminent death seemed to be looming and so I wanted to think of other things. And what was there to think about except the life I had lived? I took comfort in memories, but the memories were jumbled, selective, rose-coloured, unstable, more like fragments of dreams, but their unifying impulse was the feel of Lárochka's light body on my chest and the solace of a human embrace.

Maybe I was close to delirium as my mind ranged more widely and more wildly. The unceasing onslaught of the screaming wind, hour after hour, without the least respite, invited an escape into madness. The physical world had become insane, so why not join in the party? What good now were reticence and orderliness? Why not let my mind go its own way for once, without constraint? As I abandoned myself to a procession of random thoughts and images, each of them pulling me further and further into a make-believe world, I felt warmer and happier and more relaxed.

*

A new element within the texture of all the conflicting noises slowly penetrated my dream-state and brought me back to the awful present. I knew that sound well enough – loose sailcloth flapping.

*Oh God!*

I dragged myself back into sailor mode, knowing exactly what had happened without even looking. The lashing holding the sail bundle to its gallows had come loose and the leech of the sail was now free to flap furiously in the wind and would soon destroy itself in the process. Worse, if the lashing failed completely, there was a risk of the sail fanning up from its after end – effectively setting some sail. That didn't bear thinking about. I had to sort out the problem immediately.

It was a struggle to get myself upright. My legs were stiff and cold, and I had to let Lárochka down as gently as possible as I stood up. Pleased that I had kept my waterproofs on, I put the hood of my jacket up and tightened the toggle on my hat. I opened the hatch and stuck my head out.

*Jesus!*

It was an abrupt, almost shocking transition from my idle daydreaming. A solid wall of white spray, perhaps ten or fifteen feet high, driven on by a wind that, for all I knew, may by now have been exceeding storm force, hurtled relentlessly from astern. I turned my back to it and climbed a couple more steps so that I could reach the errant lashing. I had to be careful, when re-doing it, not to allow any slack into the loops around the sail bundle. If the wind got any real purchase on even a small patch of sail, it could easily wrench the whole lot out of my grip. I knew that should that happen, I would have no chance of retrieving a sail that was in effect setting itself. I worked slowly and methodically, and once the sail had quietened down again, I reached below to grab a spare line from the shelf behind the companionway steps and doubled up on the lashing.

All the while I was working, my focus was on the sail bundle, the lashing and my hands. Once finished, I allowed myself a couple of seconds to look at the wider scene. I really did not want to, but a kind of morbid curiosity got the better of me. I was unlikely to experience anything of this ferocity again, so I may as well take a proper look before dropping back down into the cabin. I scanned the horizon ahead, to the north.

*Bloody hell!*

The sky was a low, grey mass, its finer detailing distorted by the almost solid spindrift, but away on the port bow, to our north-west, and low over the horizon, I could make out a glowing, luminous streak of cloud.

*Jesus!*

I knew exactly what it was. I had seen that same flat saucer shape and that same unnatural luminosity to the east of Svalbard, when sailing near the island of Kvitøya. It was ice blink – the light reflected off solid ice back to the underside of the cloud cover.

*Jesus Christ Almighty!*

For a second or two I was unable to move. More than anything, I had feared the prospect of us being carried into ice, and here was that prospect, now made real. At least the ice blink was not dead ahead, but that did not mean that we would be spared an encounter with less concentrated ice.

*Jesus!*

I forced myself to snap out of the terror that had immobilised me, dropped back down into the cabin and shut the hatch firmly behind me. I wiped myself down with a towel and re-settled myself and Lárochka into our tandem position on the cabin sole.

As I put my arms around her once more, I realised how important her presence had become. She was all I had to hold on to.

*Lárochka…can you hear me? Lárochka? Bad news, I'm afraid. There's ice somewhere ahead to the north-west. We're not heading straight for it, luckily, but things don't look good. There could be ice anywhere now. And with this wind and the drogue set, there's absolutely nothing I can do. Nothing at all. We're in a bind, Lárochka, but I'll look after you to the end. That I promise. I promise…I promise.*

I settled back to my dream state, or tried to, but it was impossible. Before, the idea of running into ice had been no more than an abstract possibility. Now, that prospect lay somewhere between a probability and a certainty. Before, I could entertain the idea that if everything held, this storm might be survivable. Now, with this new element firmly in the equation, that idea of survival seemed increasingly fanciful. We were now being pushed steadily north towards an almost certain death and my daydreaming took on an altogether different complexion.

Every time I closed my eyes, I heard the crash as we were flung onto an icefloe, shattering *M.'s* hull. I felt the rush of frigid water into the cabin, the shock of that sudden immersion, the terror that I was about to die. I knew that I would not drown, that I would be killed by hypothermia in a matter of minutes. We are told that death by cold is a peaceful death, that the urge is to sleep, that one drifts gently off into quietus. We are told, too, that a life is as long as it is destined to be, and that the wise man accepts his fate without screams or blubbering. I thought of the countless sailors who have drowned over the centuries, many of them in waters as cold as this. How did they face their final seconds? Did they fight or did they concede without a struggle? I thought of Tilman, an old man like me, drowned in the South Atlantic. When his ship went down and he knew it was the end, did he feel fear, or anger, or possibly relief that at last it was all over? I wondered whether it mattered anyway. The only judge of how I handled those final seconds would be me, and my judgement would be extinguished even more quickly than my body. The man kneeling at the guillotine in the public square has some motivation to conduct himself with composure and hide his terror. But here, in the wastes of the Arctic, there would be no witness were I to die an abject, cowardly death. Nobody would know, and chances were, too, that nobody would ever know what happened to *M.* and her skipper. *He disappeared somewhere up north. He was a fool, anyway, making those voyages in those crazy yachts. It was bound to end badly.* The singlehanded sailor always risks a lonely death. Not for him or her a *holy, clean and in-between-the-sheets* death, soothed by soft whispering and caresses. My eyes moistened as I thought about my family, my partner, my son and daughter, my grandchildren. I would never see them again, never laugh with them again. I really did not want to leave them. It was too cruel. Mortality is too cruel. Inevitable, yes, but cruel too. You are part of this great construct for decade after decade, then boom! just like that, it's over. Everything given and everything taken away.

I gripped Lárochka more tightly and another thought struck me. Nobody would ever know that we had died together. Our respective fates would never be linked. Two sailors lost in the Arctic, but with nothing to connect them. This story was our story and ours alone. Even that was not quite correct, as Lárochka had never been anything but an unconscious participant in the story. I had no idea whether anything had registered with her since I had found her. I liked to think so, but it seemed improbable.

*Lárochka. I know you probably can't hear me or understand what I am saying, but I must talk to you. You're now the only person I have. Everyone else is gone, left behind. So many people, so many lives, so many stories. All gone. There's just you and me and however many minutes we have left. How do we pass the time? I think I'll sing to you for a while. That would make me feel better. I remember singing in the sea after abandoning ship many years ago. We had the whole crew, fourteen of us, I think, roped together around a big rubber ring. We sang all the shanties we knew. It gave us the courage to hold on.*

> *In South Australia I was born*
> *Heave away! Haul Away!*
> *South Australia round Cape Horn*
> *Bound for South Australia!*

Tears ran down my cheeks. God, that was all so long ago! We all should have drowned then but didn't.

> *Wish I was in a foreign land*
> *Heave away! Haul away!*
> *Bottle of whisky in my hand*
> *Bound for South Australia!*

> *As we wallop around Cape Horn*
> *Heave away! Haul away!*
> *Wish to God you'd never been born*
> *Bound for South Australia!*

For the first time in many years, I remembered my shipmates. It was the bosun, Spinger, who was the shantyman and who had started up the refrain in the cold water of the Pacific. Where was he now? Where were the rest of them? How had their lives been? We were all young and just starting out. So much energy and hope and expectation. Soon it would all be extinguished.

I sang Lárochka another song of the sea that I had known all my life, a Russian one this time.

*Тот кто рождён был у море*
*Тот полюбил навсегда*
*Белые мачты на рейде*
*В дымке морской города*

*Whoever is born by the sea*
*Forever falls in love*
*With the white masts in the anchorage*
*Of the misty seaside cove*

*Свет маяка над волною*
*Южных ночей забытьё*
*Самое синее в мире*
*Чёрное море моё, чёрное море моё*

*The beam of the lighthouse over the waves*
*The summer nights' eternity*
*The bluest sea in the world*
*My own Black Sea, my own Black Sea*

It has a beautiful, haunting melody, this song, in a minor mode, filling it with sadness and longing. It was too much to bear. I stopped singing.

*Ah, Lárochka, Lárochka. It makes me too sad, this song. I could sing you something happier, but what's the point? Maybe I'll be quiet for a while.*

I was terrified of falling asleep. I knew that it would make no difference in the long run, but I wanted to be awake and alert when we hit the ice. Who knows, maybe just a few seconds of action might be enough to avert the inevitable. Ha! Avert the inevitable! Yes, it was illogical, irrational, but I was not yet ready to concede.

I clung on to wakefulness, hour after hour. The wind continued to wail, and the drogue yo-yoed us on and on. I ate an energy bar followed by an apple, the last meal of the condemned man. My eyelids drooped and my jaw went slack. I shook myself. *No! No! You mustn't sleep! Stay awake, for God's sake! It's your only hope! Stay awake! Stay awake!*

## 33

It was a harsh light irritating my eyelids that eventually woke me. It came and went, this beam of brightness, on and off, in an irregular pattern, and slowly, ever so slowly, pulled me back to some level of consciousness. Something was flashing in my face. My inner mind, dead to the world, wanted to ignore it, wanted to stay wrapped in the cocoon of profound sleep that it had at last woven around itself. Sleep was its protection against the assaults of the world, and it did not want to budge. It ignored this insistent flashing, with the wisdom of the subconscious. Here, in deepest sleep, the mind was unassailable. This bothersome intrusion from the outside world could only presage something bad, and so it ignored it. For how long, I have no idea. Maybe minutes, maybe hours. The flashing merged into my dreams, became part of them. Orange flashes, sometimes a few seconds apart, sometimes longer. For a long time, I absorbed them and diverted them, unable and unwilling to let them force me back to consciousness.

Even when the insistence of this flashing became impossible to resist, it took a long, long time to reascend from the depths of sleep to something approaching wakefulness. I lay there, eyes closed, aware that something was irritating my eyelids, but without the least awareness of where I was or what might be the cause of that irritation. All I knew was that I was in a state of profound peace and that I did not want to break the spell. Wherever I was, it was calm and still, and I wanted the moment to last forever.

The insistent flashing finally induced me, against my will, to half-open my eyes. A blinding light forced them shut again. The flashing stopped and I opened my eyes once more. Above me was the salt-stained glass of *M.'s* hatch, with its protective aluminium bars. It took me a little while to establish that I must be at sea. The boat rolled ever so slightly, bringing the sun into alignment with my eyes and once more blinding me. The sun must be nearly overhead. The sun? And why was everything so calm and quiet? I struggled through into wakefulness, not understanding anything. Why was I on the cabin sole with my head bent back onto a companionway step? What was this weight on my chest?

I finally shook off the profound torpor that had disabled my brain and my memory and clawed my way slowly back to the real world. Yes, I was at sea. Of course. It was a calm, clear day and the sun was peeking through the hatch each time we rolled. The rolling was very gentle, just a few degrees each way. Something still did not make sense. I forced my way back to full cognition and now remembered everything. The liferaft.

Lárochka. The storm. The storm? Now I remembered that I had done all I could not to fall asleep. Exhaustion must have got the better of me. I must have slept for a long, long time. I looked at my watch and tried to calculate how long I had slept for. As far as I can recall, it was something like fifteen hours.

I lay my head back onto the companionway step and closed my eyes again. I was rested and relieved and the sun was shining on what must have been a calm sea. It was so peaceful, there in the cabin with just the faintest lapping of water against the hull. We had not hit ice. The storm had gone. The tensions of the previous days drained away.

During sleep, my arms had fallen to my sides. I put them around Lárochka to celebrate our escape and knew instantly that she was dead. Something in the stiffness and immobility of her body was unmistakable. I could have tried to feel for a pulse, or held a mirror to her lips, but I knew there was no point. Lárochka was dead. The tiny spark that had somehow kept her alive for all that time had been extinguished. Unable to maintain her weak hold on the thin thread of her life, she had died while I slept.

*Oh no... Lárochka.*

I cradled her in my arms and once more buried my nose in the fur of her shapka. The sun played over her face, tracing little circular patterns around her chin and cheeks. I could easily have closed my eyes and fallen asleep again. It was a long time since I had known such peace.

Now that I think back to that moment, trying to recreate it as well as I can, I am surprised by the sense of calm that flooded through me after finding that Lárochka had died. I felt a deep, unspeakable grief, yes, and the first gnawings of guilt for having been unable to save her, but these dark feelings were, for the moment, more than offset by the relief of having, yet again, survived a seemingly impossible situation. It is likely, too, that somewhere deep down I acknowledged that Lárochka's death had released me from the race to get her to Longyearbyen in time, a race which I already knew I could not win. Her death had become increasingly inevitable, one way or the other. At least the question of how and when she would die had been resolved. Added to all of that was the utter stillness of the moment, a stillness enhanced by its contrast with the hellish fury in which I had fallen asleep.

It would have been so easy to have closed my eyes and drifted off again, but I resisted the temptation, stood up and lifted Lárochka's body back onto the bunk as gently as I could. Her eyes had opened and for a second time I saw those deep blue irises staring unseeingly at a world now dead to her. I closed each of her eyelids and kissed her cheek. It was icy cold.

I stared at her face. Death had not yet robbed her of her beauty. I studied her delicate features. This was the first time that I had been alone with a dead person, but I had spent so much time with an impassive Lárochka that the change in her condition was, in one sense, no more than a small shift: she didn't look much different than she had for the whole time since I had found her. But now she was dead, and everything had changed.

*Lárochka, I'm so sorry. I did all I could, but it wasn't enough. I wish we could have changed places. It was you who should have survived, not an old man like me. I don't understand this world. So much senselessness. So much pain. How can your beautiful body be snuffed out like this? How can your flesh and your life be so worthless? How can fate be so casual? I know it sounds stupid, but I will always love you, Lárochka. I'll love you as the girl I never knew. As the girl who died in my arms in an Arctic storm. I'll love you as the beautiful Arctic tern, too, so wild and free. You will stay in my heart until my own death, Lárochka, that I promise.*

I lashed the bunk straps tight, to keep Lárochka's body in place. I knew that I would have to think about what to do with her but pushed that thought away for the moment. There was a much more pressing priority: I had to see what was going on outside. I still couldn't make sense of the change in conditions while I had been sleeping. Everything seemed so unlikely that for a few seconds I was reluctant to open the hatch, fearful of what I might find.

*OK. Let's go!*

I undogged the hatch handles, pushed the hatch forward to its open position and climbed a few steps up the companionway ladder.

*Bloody hell!*

All around was a scene of terrifying, incandescent beauty: an unblemished pale-blue sky, a piercing sun, a deep indigo sea and, stretching to every horizon, a patchwork of fantastical, unworldly, blindingly brilliant ice floes.

*Jesus!*

How in the name of God had we ended up in the middle of this lot? And more to the point, how in the name of God would we get out?

I checked over the boat.

*Bloody hell!*

I had completely forgotten about the series drogue.

It took a minute or two, standing there in the hatchway, to organise my mind and adjust to this startling new reality. Lárochka was dead, the drogue was no doubt hanging straight down off the stern and needed retrieving as soon as possible, and we were becalmed on a flat sea amongst ice. Unbelievable. All I could assume was that the storm had passed before we had encountered the ice and that we had subsequently been encircled by the drifting floes. Had the density of the floes been much greater, we would almost certainly have collided with one by now, but we had somehow stayed in clear water. The sea was now so flat, no doubt largely due to the calming effect of the ice, that even if we nudged a floe, we might not be damaged. I preferred to not put that to the test.

I ducked down below and knelt beside Lárochka.

*I'm going to have to leave you again, Lárochka. I won't be too long. I've got to pull the drogue up and repack it in its bins. It's sunny and calm out there, so it won't be too hard a job. We're surrounded by ice. Not solid pack-ice, just floes. Smallish ones. Luckily, they're well-spaced. I wish you could see them. They're so amazing to look at. They're kind of sculpted into the most incredible shapes and patterns. I can even feel a little bit of warmth from the sun, too. I can't believe how things have changed since I fell asleep. Anyway, I've got to go.*

I slipped on my harness, pulled myself up on deck and began my work. In essence it was the launching of the drogue in reverse: pulling the line aboard and coiling it on the after deck, followed by packing it back into its bins, unhitching it from its bridle, taking the bridle back over the self-steering gear, unlashing the steering pendulum and letting it rotate back into the water, uncoiling the control lines for the self-steering and resetting them into their cleats on the bridge deck.

I now had a sailable yacht again but, for the moment anyway, no wind to sail in and a dangerously congested sea. I also had a dead passenger.

# 34

By now, this voyage had moved so far outside the realm of what I thought possible, that I was increasingly beset by a feeling of unreality. I seemed to have lost all control of what was happening and become a mere pawn. Every time I tried to do the right thing and insert an element of self-determination into the proceedings, I was hit by yet another unthinkable crisis. I had wandered into a universe *where Destiny with Men for Pieces plays.* There was something of the cosmic joker, too, about this chap *Destiny.* Was I being mocked? Was my endless discomfort purely for the amusement of some malign deity? Or was this all a test, a trial by storm, ice and death? Was I being pushed to the limits to see whether my spirit would hold strong? And what about Lárochka? How did she fit into this cosmic game? It was only by the most unlikely of chances that I had seen her liferaft. If I had not seen it, how might things have worked out? I have no doubt that Lárochka would have died, probably sooner than she eventually did. I thought about my own trajectory and realised with a jolt that Lárochka may have saved my life. Had I not found her, I would not have made those several days of easting before being hit by the storm. I would almost certainly have been much further to the north-west towards the solid ice indicated by the iceblink I had seen. Lárochka's inert body had forced me away from the dangerous sector I was heading into.

*Jesus!*

I sat in the hatchway for a few more minutes, turning these thoughts over and over and trying to make sense of it all. Maybe there was no sense to it. Maybe we were just the playthings of an endless blind causality, an ever-spinning roulette of pure chance. I realised that there was a bitter irony at play here: in trying to save Lárochka, I had unwittingly saved myself. Lárochka had saved me and now she was dead.

Despite the long sleep from which I had only recently awoken, I was still exhausted and neither ready to start sailing again nor to think too deeply about Lárochka. Nevertheless, having acknowledged that I owed her much more than she owed me, I was drawn back to her side. She now meant even more to me. I knelt beside her.

*Lárochka…if I get out of this mess, it will only be because of you. I've only just realised this. If I had carried on as intended, there is virtually no chance I could have escaped being driven onto solid ice. Lárochka…you saved my life. You will never know, and I will never be able to thank you properly. That is so strange and so cruel. I hope you are at peace, wherever you are. That's the least you deserve. I'm so tired, Lárochka, so tired. I'm going to eat something and then sleep for a while longer, perhaps an hour or two. We'll get some wind sooner or later and I'll try and find a way out of here.*

I assembled and ate a quick snack, set my alarm for sixty minutes and settled on the cabin sole to sleep. I suppose that I could have moved Lárochka to the cabin sole and had the comfortable bunk for myself, but there was something indecent about that thought. She deserved the best I could give her, even in death, and for as long as she was on board, that would be her resting place.

The sun had moved lower and was now shining obliquely through the hatch, no longer troubling my face. I was asleep almost as soon as I had closed my eyes, lulled by the gentle rocking of the boat and the magnificent, overpowering silence.

✳

I dreamed of blue eyes. Not the cornflower blue of Lárochka's eyes, but a lighter, more piercing blue and, on waking, I could still hear the voice of the old man Joshua.

*Ye take care. Ye take care.*

I had not thought of him or his gentle warning since Jan Mayen. *Ye take care.* Given all that had happened, those three words had now assumed an unlikely weightiness. They could have been nothing more than a polite formula, said without meaning or intent, but the stress he had put on them and the accompanying stare suggested that they were a specific warning of some sort. My tendency is towards rational thought, and so I rejected the idea that this stranger Joshua had some knowledge or premonition about what was going to happen on this voyage. That was nonsense. Nonetheless, the questions remained. Who the hell was he? Why did he warn me?

The extra hour of sleep had revived me considerably and I now felt ready to confront the next challenges: bringing my navigation up to date, constructing a strategy for getting clear of the ice, and deciding what to do about Lárochka. There had been no change in the conditions while I slept. The sun was now low on the northern horizon and the sea was as smooth as ever. The ice floes around us had shifted their relative positions, but only slightly. As far as I could tell from my hand-held GPS, the current here was flowing at about half a knot to the west-south-west. With no wind to influence speed or direction, everything on the water, *M.* included, was moving along in the same parallel motion.

As far as I can recall we were roughly at 79° 30' North, 3° East, and therefore still more than two hundred miles from Longyearbyen, now to our south-east. This worked in our favour, as my preferred course out of the ice was in that same south-easterly direction. This was the quickest route back into the warmer north-flowing waters of the North Atlantic Current where, I knew from experience, there was little chance of encountering ice at this time of the year.

Having thought everything through and established the navigational parameters, the resultant plan of action was simple: once we had some wind, I would sail to the south-east, or as near as was possible to the south-east, still with the intention of taking Lárochka to Longyearbyen.

*Lárochka…I'm feeling a lot better now. I can't believe how tired I was. Once we've got some wind we'll be out of the ice and on our way to Longyearbyen. That still seems to be the best plan. They can look after you properly there.*

The skin on her face was drawn more tightly over her cheekbones and jawline, and her eyes were more sunken. She was still beautiful, but it was a more ghost-like, distant beauty. Her mouth had opened slightly, too, showing her even white teeth. I remembered something about tying a cloth around the jaw to keep it closed but left her as she was.

*Lárochka…you're going to have to hang on a while longer. I keep saying this, I know. You have been so strong up until now. We'll get you to land. Maybe we can even get you home, wherever that is. I'll do my best, anyway. Just keep going, Lárochka. I won't let you down.*

I lit the stove and cooked my first hot meal for a while, with the intention of gradually re-establishing my normal eating routine. There was now no need to keep the stove going. In fact, the opposite was true – from here on a cooler cabin might be better for Lárochka.

I sat down on the cabin sole and did my best to bring my logbooks up to date, relying largely on memory. They had become patchy, disjointed records of what had happened since we had crossed paths with the liferaft. I am usually meticulous in my record-keeping, but this recent laxity no longer troubled me. All the petty hour-by-hour details seemed less and less important. A girl had died in my arms. Did it matter whether it was at 0239 hours on this day or 1323 hours on that day? Would an accurate estimation of yesterday's noon position help to bring her back? And how could I possibly record the maelstrom of emotions I had felt over the previous few days?

I realise now that I was still shocked and still grieving, much more than I was then prepared to admit. To have tried to record what had happened, while Lárochka was still lying serenely on my bunk, would have meant confronting too many things which were at that moment beyond my capacity to understand and to verbalise. And it seemed grossly disrespectful, too, to write about Lárochka while she was there beside me. As we have seen, it would take many years before I could write about her with a relatively untroubled mind.

# 35

One of the recurring characteristics of this voyage was my capacity to make incorrect assumptions about the weather, time after time. Having, by pure luck, come through the worst storm I had ever experienced and emerged into the most benign Arctic weather imaginable, my eternal optimism clicked in once more and I foresaw us escaping the ice with the help of the inevitable light breeze that would soon get up. Had I learned nothing during the previous few days? On what basis did I think I had any ability to predict the weather hereabouts? Why was I constantly constructing ideal scenarios? Maybe it was the pressure of having Lárochka aboard, whether she was alive or dead. The usual dynamic of my sea-going had been turned on its head. As a solo sailor, I had spent years honing an indifference to what the next day's weather may be. There was nothing I could do to change it, virtually nothing I could do, in my tiny yachts, to escape it, and so by far the best strategy was to accept everything that came along with perfect equanimity.

Now, for the very first time in all my years of singlehanded ocean sailing, I was under pressure to meet a kind of fixed schedule. For several days, I had been required to be at a certain spot – Longyearbyen, by a certain time – in this case as soon as possible. It is only now that I can see how this pressure transformed my usual stoic mindset, turning imperturbability into an ill-considered optimism. I had started to believe what it suited me to believe. This is not a good mindset for a sailor.

*

Yes, I really did think that the worst was now over and that from here on everything would be, as they say, plain sailing. This is not to understate the dark shadow that Lárochka's death had cast over a large portion of my mind, a shadow that was growing in size and intensity as each hour passed.

It took several days for me to realise that the obvious danger of the storm had been replaced by a more tolerable but equally insidious threat. Under a permanent sparkling sun and a sky devoid of even the slightest hint of a wind, we were being carried further and further to the west, away from Svalbard and towards the inevitable cumulations of ice off northern Greenland. The Russians call this stretch of water between Svalbard and Greenland the Fram Strait, after Nansen's ship. The term is not much used on charts, but it has always appealed to me, as the Fram's captain, Otto Sverdrup, has long been a personal hero of mine. The irony of finding myself trapped in this strait, through lack of wind, did not escape me.

Hour after hour, I sat in the hatchway, searching the surface of the water for anything that might presage wind: a dark patch, a few catspaws. I watched the wind indicator at the masthead, hoping it might spring to life and start gyrating a little. When below I kept an eye on *M.*s ensign, now even more shredded from the recent storm, which hung down lifelessly from the top section of the mainsheet, and which I could see through the after portlight.

Our constant movement to the west was almost imperceptible, carried as we were on a broad sea, with everything else – the ice floes, the flocks of little auks dotted on the surface, our attendant fulmars, now permanently grounded in the still air - moving along in harmony with us.

There were some compensations that came with this forced inactivity. I was able to rest, albeit on the discomfort of the cabin sole, and could now eat according to my normal routine. Despite all that, I could feel a growing agitation. We were being forced away from Longyearbyen and the chances of being able to deliver Lárochka were diminishing rapidly. How long could I keep her on board? How long would it take before her body started to decompose? I had no answer to these questions, but I was beginning to accept that Longyearbyen was no longer a valid target.

*Lárochka...unless things change soon, I don't think I'm going to be able to get you to Longyearbyen. At the moment it's impossible. We're utterly becalmed and being carried to the west. God knows when we'll get some wind. Lárochka...I don't know what I'm going to do with you. This is really hard to say...but I can't keep you on board for ever. I'm sure you understand. You know, you're going to start deteriorating soon. It's not cold enough here to preserve you, or I don't think so anyway. We'll give it a bit more time, but I just wanted to warn you. I do wish I could keep you on board. I really do. I've grown very fond of you. It's nice having your company, someone to talk to, someone to think about. I imagine you're a really good sailor, too. Maybe we could have made voyages together, proper ones. I think we would have been a good team, you and I. I prefer to be on my own at sea, but maybe I would have liked sailing with you. In fact, I'm sure I would. Anyway, I'm sorry I seem to have let you down again. I hope you'll forgive me, Lárochka. I've tried my best, but nothing has gone right.*

⁎

I had sailed through widely spaced ice floes on one previous occasion, sixty miles to the east of Scoresby Sound on the east Greenland coast. That had been a magical moment, in overcast, sightly misty conditions. I had been captivated by the fantastical shapes acquired by the floes after their months of gradual melting. There had been something ghostly about those delicately filigreed but dangerous blocks of ice moving along in total silence.

The floes we were now amongst were sculpted to the same unlikely patterns, but in the brilliant sunshine they took on a quite different character. Subdued ghostliness had been replaced by a blinding, hard-shadowed self-confidence. Their constant glinting and glowing gave off an air of *joie-de-vivre;* there was something life-affirming in their dazzling whiteness. This may seem contradictory – they were nothing but blocks of ice, after all - but think of the way the heart can lift on seeing an expanse of virgin snow on a clear winter's morning. To be amongst the floes is therefore wonderful and terrifying at the same time. They are beautiful and unworldly assassins.

I can't remember exactly how long it was since waking from the storm that I started to sense a change in the density of the floes. I think a day or two had passed before it became clear that they were closing up very slightly, reducing the amount of clear water between them. This is not to say that I felt we were in any imminent danger. Had a little breeze come up, there was still plenty of space between the floes to navigate in. It was concerning, all the same, as there was a strong likelihood that this trend would increase as we moved further to the west. It also gave the lie to my impression that everything was moving along in parallel harmony. This clearly was not the case. The ice was accumulating, but at such a gradual pace that it was impossible to see exactly when or how.

I sat in the hatchway for hour after hour, entranced by the pure beauty and wildness of the icy seascape, and feeling increasingly helpless. Without a wind there was nothing I could do. Would we drift on to the west and then round to the south, pushed on by the East Greenland Current, with the ice growing more and more dense, until we were crushed? *M's* hull was relatively lightly built and was unlikely to survive any forceful encounter with ice. Her saving grace was her nimbleness and manoeuvrability, but without a wind, and without sea room, these counted for nothing.

My helplessness was not confined solely to matters of navigation. What was I going to do with Lárochka? I could not keep her on board for much longer, but I had a fierce resistance to the idea of throwing her overboard. Consider, too, that even now I refer to Lárochka as 'her' rather than 'her body'. I knew, intellectually, that she was now no more than lifeless flesh and bone and that it mattered not a jot what was done with that flesh and bone. Despite that, I could not bring myself to think of her remains as no more than dead meat to be disposed of by the most convenient method available. Perhaps this was a result of my unfamiliarity with death and the dead. I had not developed the hardened attitude of someone who deals with death regularly. I knew that Lárochka was dead, but I still thought of her as a sentient, sensitive being. My mind could feel her physical shock at being dropped into the frigid water. It was clear to me that this was irrational, perhaps even stupid, and that I was going to have to steel myself to dispose of her. I needed a little more time to accustom myself to the idea.

✳

I sat in the hatchway and watched the birds, too. Small flocks of little auks whirred around, sometimes landing on the water, sometimes taking a ride on an ice floe. Groups of kittiwakes flew north, as they always seem to do hereabouts in summer. From time to time an Iceland gull joined us, sitting off our quarter and watching us with a puzzled eye.

And then there were the Arctic terns. I watched them pass with even more interest than usual. Elegant long-winged swallows of the sea, they powered along with an energetic, bouncy flight, chattering ceaselessly to their fellow travellers. Their jaunty self-sufficiency was a rebuke to my own lumpen mode of progress. Storm or calm meant nothing to them; with just a few ounces of flesh and feathers they could traverse a whole planet. Their easy passage made me feel even more entrapped, more than ever ill-suited to these ocean wanderings.

Nonetheless, those hours of quiet observation of the ice and its wildlife did help to calm and revive me after the extreme events of the previous week. They also helped to reconcile me to the pressing need to deal with Lárochka.

# 36

I had no idea how long it would be before Lárochka's body started to decompose, or even what would happen when the process really got under way. I could already see some changes. Her eye sockets had sunk even lower and the skin on her face was becoming blotched and waxy. I had a vague memory that at some point a body starts discharging fluids. It was that as much as anything that spurred me into action.

You may think that giving someone a burial at sea is a simple matter. That may be so on a fully crewed ship, with lots of space and manpower, but the more I considered the problem, the more daunting it became. Firstly, there were the logistics – I would have to somehow get Lárochka's body up the companionway steps and through the narrow hatch. It had been difficult enough to take her down into the cabin, with gravity working in my favour. I wasn't sure whether I had the strength to pull her up the other way. Once Lárochka was on deck, I would somehow have to move her to the side deck and get her overboard.

This is where I really baulked. Yes, I could probably manage to push or throw her into the sea, but that was an unthinkable way to treat a shipmate. A proper burial at sea, as I imagined it, is no doubt a grand affair: a body sewn into a weighted canvas bag, laid out neatly on a wide board and covered with an ensign; the crew lined up, caps off, in respectful silence; some pertinent words and a prayer or two from the ship's chaplain; maybe a hymn sung by the assembled company; the board gently upended and the body consigned to the deep with full and appropriate honours. That's how a burial at sea should be, and it looked like I was going to be unable to reproduce even one single element of such a ceremony.

*Lárochka...Lárochka. I'm so sorry, Lárochka, but you're not going to be able to stay much longer. God knows, I'd like to keep you on board, but it's impossible. I'm going to have to bury you. Into the sea, of course. I suppose that's fitting for a sailor and an Arctic tern, but all the same, I wish I didn't have to do it. Look, Lárochka, it's going to be a bit rough. I've got to get you up through the hatch. I'll be as gentle as I can, I promise. And then into the sea. I think I've worked out how to do it as respectfully as I can. I just want you to know that I'll be doing my best for you, even if it doesn't feel that way. I don't know how I'm going to cope, once you've gone. I've never felt lonely at sea, but I've grown so used to having you with me that I know I'm really going to miss you. That's pretty stupid, I suppose, but there we are. Things are still a bit awkward out there, which doesn't help. I'm not at all sure I'll be able to get out of the ice. It's getting thicker, bit by bit, and we're still being pushed the wrong way. Ha! Maybe I'll be joining you in a day or two. Anyway, I've just got to prepare a few things and then we'll start. I just wanted you to know that I'm doing the best I can.*

*

I had decided that I would bury her as she now was, wearing the clothes I had put on her – my clothes. There was little choice, anyway, but I liked the idea of her taking something of mine to her final resting place. In particular, I was happy to bequeath her my beautiful hand-knitted Faroese fisherman's sweater, my most prized sea-going item of clothing. It suited her extraordinarily well, even in death. I decided, too, to pull her seaboots on over the socks I had given her, to help weight her down once in the water.

I carry several anchors on board, even though they are rarely used, and I pulled the heaviest out from its stowage place aft, along with its short length of galvanised chain. This would serve as a weight to take Lárochka down quickly and hold her in the depths. There was something unseemly in the idea of her floating on the surface, prey for surface scavengers. I lifted the anchor and chain through the hatch and placed them in the cockpit, ready for when I needed them.

I retrieved Lárochka's harness, buckled it tightly onto her, and looped a spare line under the two shoulder straps. Apart from the final task of once more slackening off the starboard lifeline, the physical preparations were complete.

I tore an empty page from the back of my logbook, took a pen from the pen rack and sat down on the cabin sole. Using the logbook to rest the paper on, I began writing. It took me a long while to compose a funeral oration in the best Russian I could muster. My writing was no doubt full of basic errors, but for this final act of farewell it seemed important to use Lárochka's native language. I knew well enough that this was irrational, but since when were ritual and ceremony based on reason alone? This was as much for me as for her. I knew that I would feel considerably better for having made the effort to send her off in Russian. And even if the overall sense of what I was saying was somewhat opaque, the Slavic sound and intonation of the words would be much more appropriate. I searched around in the recesses of my memory, winkling out phrases and long-forgotten fragments that might give some weight to my words. I thought of her tattoo – *Свобода/ Freedom* – and tried to work in something apposite. The Russian for Arctic tern escaped me completely, but I got around that problem with *твоя самая любимая птица/your favourite bird*, confident that she would know what I meant.

Once I was as satisfied as I could be with what I had written, I stuffed the sheet into the pocket of my waterproof jacket, stood up and launched into the task I had been dreading - getting Lárochka out of the cabin and onto the side deck.

I won't dwell too much on the detail. In essence I had to line her body up on the cabin sole, climb out of the hatch and then, using the line through her harness shoulder straps, pull her up and far enough through the hatch to be able to I lower her torso back over the after hatch coaming. In this position she was half in and half out of the hatch, lying back somewhat awkwardly. From there it was a matter of manoeuvring her fully out and onto the starboard side deck. It was hard work and were it not for the flat sea I doubt that I would have been able to do it. I still could not rid myself of the notion that I was hurting her with all this rough handling. I'm not ashamed of this and in retrospect I think it is a good thing. I prefer to be over-sensitive rather than the opposite, and in any case, how are we to know what the dead are and aren't aware of? Although I don't have any personal belief in any kind of afterlife beyond the reabsorption of our atoms into the fabric of the world, I fully accept that I may be quite wrong about this.

Once Lárochka was on the side deck, or more precisely, lying partly on the cockpit coaming and partly on the spare steering oar lashed to the side deck, I went below and brought out the anchor and chain. I laid the anchor along her thighs and wrapped the chain round her legs and the anchor shank several times, passing it through the crotch straps of her harness as I went and finishing off with a few half hitches around the harness straps. With the anchor well secured to Lárochka, I moved aft and for the second time on this voyage untied the lashing that tensions the lifeline. All the preparations had been made. Here amongst the ice in the north-west corner of the Greenland Sea, I was about to conduct my first burial at sea.

*

I sat down for a while on the narrow bridge deck, to give myself a few minutes to get my breath back and to clear my head for what I was about to do. Lárochka was dead, but there was something so final and irrevocable about committing her body to the sea that I was still hesitant. I wasn't sure, either, whether I had the right, legal or otherwise, to perform this act. When I had decided that I had no choice but to bury Lárochka, everything had seemed straightforward, but now that the moment had arrived, I felt much less confident. For the first time, I started to suspect that this story was untellable. *A solo British sailor picks up a Russian girl in a liferaft, she dies, and he buries her at sea.* The more I thought about it, the more I realised that it was a story that opened itself up to a whole gamut of questions and misinterpretations. I had done my best in difficult circumstances, but I was experienced enough in the ways of the world to know how even the most innocent story can be twisted to suit the ravenous and unprincipled maw of the media, and how an army of armchair critics and advice-givers would soon get to work.

I pushed all that aside, for the moment anyway, and concentrated on Lárochka. Her face, its heavily blotched skin now darkening, showed only the very last hints of her beauty. Despite that, the Faroese sweater with its high roll neck, along with the fur shapka, still gave her a jaunty, coquettish look. I wondered yet again whether she was just as I imagined her, or an altogether different person. I would never know. She had come out of nowhere, this stranger, and now she was about to disappear for ever.

I stood up in the cockpit and looked around. Everything sparkled under a low sun. Everything was either blue or a brilliant, blinding white. The silence was total. I knew that even if I did not survive, I was lucky to experience such a scene. We were in the very heart of wildness, Lárochka and I. Time and space had dissolved away. There was only this one unending moment. I pulled my sheet of paper from my pocket and began to read what I had written. As ever, I felt shy, talking alone to the universe, but as I went on my confidence grew and I declaimed my words more strongly, raising my voice so that it would be heard to the ends of the blue and to the ends of the brilliant, blinding white.

*I stand here today to honour the life of Lárochka. I know that were it possible this ceremony would be attended by a multitude of loving family and friends, for I have no doubt whatsoever that Lárochka was loved by all who knew her. And I know that they would all, to a man and woman, be devastated by her untimely death. This is only natural, and it is right to grieve, but every life has its own shape and its own duration. I think it was Seneca who said that nobody dies too soon, as it was not their destiny to live longer than they did. I know that this is hard to accept, but don't forget that relative to the infinity of time, every single life, however long, is no more than the briefest spark. Perhaps it is selfish and ungrateful to want anything more than we are given. We should celebrate our lives, but also be ready to celebrate our deaths.*

*I am, I admit, the least qualified to talk about Lárochka and her life. I have only known her for a few days. We have never exchanged a meaningful word. In one sense I know nothing about her apart from her name, but despite that, I feel an affinity and an affection for her. I have no idea how she came to be in the liferaft I found, but the very fact of being in a liferaft in the Greenland Sea tells me that she was exceptional and adventurous. Maybe she too was a singlehanded sailor. I don't know and perhaps I will never know, but that is not important. What I do know is that she felt strongly enough about her favourite bird to have one tattooed on her arm, along with the word Freedom. The more I think about this, the more it impresses me. Lárochka clearly knew a lot about nature, and maritime nature in particular. I cannot imagine that she did not know that her favourite bird flies a longer distance than any other bird, that it is equally at home in both hemispheres, that it is as fearless as it is elegant. Maybe Lárochka aspired to those same qualities.*

I was no longer reading my notes, seized as I was by a rush of untypical eloquence. My Russian was no doubt garbled and ungrammatical, but the sounds were now no more than an outward expression of my thoughts, which were themselves crystal clear. Many of the Russian words were made up on the spot, rough equivalents and clumsy neologisms, incomprehensible to a listener, but I knew what I meant. It was, literally, the thought that counted. In a strange way I began to enjoy this terrible moment. Days of accumulated tension were released as I shouted my oration to the ice floes and to the sky and to any creature thereabouts that cared to listen. My words were for Lárochka and for her life and for her death, but they became, too, an assertion of myself and my own tenuous hold on existence. They said: *I am here! Yes, I too am nothing. I too will soon go the way of Lárochka, but for the moment I am here! Listen to me! Listen to my voice! I too can make noise!*

I continued on, now improvising fluently.

*Today we are burying Lárochka, just one amongst us, but let this be a rehearsal for all our deaths and all our burials. Lárochka's body will soon be at the depths of the ocean, but one way or another we'll all be joining her before long. There is no escape. Hey! You ice floes! You're dying too! You'll soon be melting away to nothing! And you – the sea! Don't think you'll escape either! Your time will come when the sun flairs and you boil away to nothing! And you – the sun! Don't be so sure of yourself! You won't last either! And do you think I care! The wonder and nonsense of it all!*

I stopped for a moment. When the words came again, they came quietly.

*Anyway, Lárochka…Lárochka…you are as much the sun and the seas and the icefloes and I will never forget you. You taught me so much during our brief friendship. I don't want you to go. I don't want to see you disappear for ever into this cold, cold water. But now I have to do it. You'll never know how much it pains me to bury you like this.*

I stood astride her body and lifted her legs round so that her calves were over the side of the boat. I pulled her torso upright with the line taken through her harness shoulder straps and continued lifting her until she was almost vertical, just over the side of the boat. I felt a sudden need for a prayer.

*Holy Lord, Holy Godhead, Holy Whoever you may be, if you are anything at all, I commit the body of dear Lárochka to your safekeeping, whatever that may be. If she has a soul or a spirit or an afterlife of some sort, then look after her with the love and attention she deserves. That is all I ask. Amen. As for you, dear Lárochka, I wish you bon voyage. Do not be too hard on me. Although I failed, I did my best. I will never forget you for a moment.*

I started to lower her into the sea, gripping the doubled line in both hands. I felt the shock as her feet disappeared under the surface and had to fight the urge to pull her back up, to keep her warm.

*Keep going! Keep going!*

I eased the rope through my hands until she was up to her mid-thighs in water.

*Oh God!*

It was unbearable, to see her body disappearing this way.

I felt as if I were murdering her in cold blood. I needed to soothe myself, to make everything alright. I found myself singing, loudly, strongly, defiantly.

> Тот кто рождён был у море
> Тот полюбил навсегда
> Белые мачты на рейде
> В дымке морской города

> *Whoever is born by the sea*
> *Forever falls in love*
> *With the white masts in the anchorage*
> *Of the misty seaside cove*

> Свет маяка над волною
> Южных ночей забытьё
> Самое синее в мире
> Чёрное море моё, чёрное море моё

> *The beam of the lighthouse over the waves*
> *The summer nights' eternity*
> *The bluest sea in the world*
> *My own Black Sea, my own Black Sea*

I sang the refrain over and over, slowly easing the rope through my hands. I am not a man who cries much, if ever, but now my eyes filled and overflowed.

Lárochka was now up to her shoulders in water which, as I looked straight down into it in the shadow of the hull, had turned from blue to black.

*Oh God!*

I was going to have to lower her head into the water. I could have let the rope go to submerge her quickly, but the thought of dropping her into the water was still intolerable.

*Keep going! Keep going!*

With an effort of will I eased the rope a few more inches until just her fur hat was showing. I had a sudden thought: should I have kept her hat, or something, as a memento?

*No! No! Keep going! Keep going!*

I sang again, to give me strength and to chase off my anguish and reluctance at what I was doing. I could now scarcely bear to look over the side. The top of Lárochka's hat was almost out of sight under the surface.

I stopped singing and held onto the rope for a few more seconds, steeling myself for the final release.

*Lárochka...I'm so sorry. Farewell.*

I pulled the two bites of the married rope apart and let one go. The loose end ran down into water and within a second or two lost its tension. I pulled the rope in.

*Jesus Christ Almighty!*

It was done. Lárochka was gone. I sat down on the bridge deck. It took a moment for the real grief to start, but once begun, I sobbed a lifetime's worth of tears. I sobbed for Lárochka and for myself and for the whole damn wonderful awfulness of every damn thing. I have no idea how long I cried for. Maybe five minutes, maybe an hour, maybe a week. I don't know. I just cried and cried, on and on. That's how it was and I had never in my life known anything like it.

# 37

Imagine the loneliness when I returned to the cabin. I had my space back, yes. I would be able to stretch out fully on my bunk and sleep comfortably, yes. I could resume all my routines to suit the rhythms of nobody other than myself, yes. I now had no imperatives save that of somehow saving myself, yes. But my cabin had become a bleak, empty, almost hateful place. Lárochka was gone. The body that I had held so tightly was gone.

I did stretch out on my bunk and sleep, but I woke to the same emptiness, the same overwhelming loneliness. The sun still sparkled on a calm blue sea and the ice floes still glowed, but all that beauty now oppressed rather than captivated. I had become a prisoner, condemned to the most solitary of confinements. I could not shake off the image of Lárochka's fur hat descending slowly beneath the surface of that black and icy water, nor could I rid myself of the notion that I had somehow murdered her, that by lowering her into the sea it was I who had extinguished her life once and for all.

I slept again, hoping thereby to escape this waking torment, and was woken by the guttural cries of an Arctic tern, forcing me to the hatch to investigate. Three terns were hovering around the masthead, with one trying to land on the flat top of the masthead fitting. This was not so unusual; terns and kittiwakes often attempt to land on the boat and over the years there have been many attempts to settle on the masthead, none of them successful as it usually moves around far too much. This time was the exception. The sea was so flat and the air so still that the tern was able to complete the manoeuvre. For a few seconds the tern's two companions swooped and played around the masthead, chattering gleefully – *kirrik kirrik kirrik*. The bird which had landed took off again and the trio resumed its northwards track, leaving me to languish in my unwelcome solitude.

*

I was tired, so tired, and even though I was now able to sleep whenever I wanted, I could not shake off a dangerous listlessness. I had become disinterested in the voyage, careless of my own safety and survival. Once or twice, we edged very close to ice floes and I watched them with a blank mind, unconcerned as to whether we might collide or not. I had descended into those cool, dark depths along with Lárochka. Maybe I should have weighted myself too and gone down with her in a last embrace. I envied her the eternal peace and forgetfulness she now enjoyed. I wanted to be there rather than here. And as far as 'here' was concerned, what did it matter whether one was at this latitude or that latitude, travelling in this direction or that direction? *Well, you know, I didn't just sail my boat to 79 degrees north, I sailed it all the way to 80 degrees north!* Ha! So what? What did any of that matter when I could picture, with alarming clarity, Lárochka's body spiralling gently down to its resting place on the bed of the Greenland Sea? I could see her settling on her back, just as she was on my bunk, her mouth slightly open, a few blonde curls still showing under her shapka. It was a sad, beautiful image – a girl lying at peace in the ocean depths, and for a long while it was all I could think of.

*

It may have been the return of the wind that helped to pull me out the torpor into which I had fallen. The wind is, after all, the lifeblood of the sailor. The longer one has been becalmed, the greater the reviving influence of a flow of sailable air. I have no precise memory of how long we had been without even a hint of a breeze, but it was a long time – four days perhaps, or maybe longer.

It was a slight ruffling of the ship's ensign that alerted me to the change. I had, for the moment, given up my usual practice of sitting in the hatchway to watch the world. My mind was elsewhere. The sea and the ice floes had become hateful, their taunting brilliance enough to sicken a man who was trying to reconcile himself to the endless and inevitable snuffing out of the light.

I had got up from my bunk for some mundane reason and my eye was drawn by a slight movement of the ensign visible through the after portlight. I looked more closely. The flag lifted slightly and swung back. I checked the tail of light cloth taped to the aft end of the wind vane. It too was showing signs of life. Something was going on. I opened the hatch and assumed my watch position. The sea was patched with darker circles of tiny catspaws tiptoeing in from the east.

*Jesus! Some wind!*

It was not remotely a sailing breeze, and it may well fade away to nothing, but it was a start. I stretched out on my bunk once more to ponder the situation. Some wind! It seemed to be coming from the east, but I knew well enough that at the end of a calm the breeze can start up from almost any quarter and can take a while to settle into its true direction. The implications of having some wind were manifold. The rate and direction of drift of everything on the surface would be considerably altered. We would no longer be moving along in unison with the floes, and this would create much more danger. There was then the unanswerable question of where the wind would settle, if it did come in, and just as importantly, how strong it would be. Would the breeze be in a good direction for helping me find a way out of the ice? Would it blow up robustly, creating something of a sea even here amongst the floes and worsening the potential outcome should we collide with any ice? It was clear that this wind, when it arrived, would be either a lifeline or a death sentence.

*

I returned to the hatchway to watch the world and consider my fate. One wind might save me; another wind might doom me. It was ever thus – all a matter of chance. I thought of Lárochka. Chance had brought me to her; that chance meeting had almost certainly saved me from being already wrecked in the ice; and now, once again, my life was about to be weighed on the scales of pure randomness. I could say that I owed my life to Lárochka, and in a very narrow sense that may have been true, but in the wider scheme of things it was nonsense: the point in time and space at which our trajectories had crossed was the result of an infinite number of causes and effects spanning an infinite expanse of time. If I had not come across Lárochka's liferaft, I would probably have been dead by now, but what about Lárochka? Yes, she almost certainly would have died, but what if she had been found by another vessel rather than by me? A ship with all the right facilities? A cruise ship with medical personnel on board, or a vessel with satellite communications? In that scenario, might she have been saved? By plucking her out of her liferaft, had I denied her the possibility of being rescued by someone more able to deal with her?

It was a terrible thought, even though I knew that I had absolutely no choice but to do what I had done. I could not have left her in the liferaft; there was at least a chance that by transferring her to *M*. I could have saved her, while there was only an infinitely small possibility that she would be found by any other vessel.

I had nothing to reproach myself with, but I nevertheless felt uneasy. Lárochka was dead. The machinations of fate had forced her into my path, and I had been unable to save her. I could not see what I could have done differently, but maybe that pointed to my own inadequacy. Maybe there was some simple procedure that could have revived her, of which I was ignorant. Maybe. Maybe. So many maybes. So many little moral dilemmas thrown up by what at first seemed a simple act of assistance.

*

I see from my computer that I have now written nearly 50,000 words about this voyage. Where are they coming from? I started out with the intention of writing a short expiatory summary of what happened, but the more I delve into it the more it grows. I had thought that by working from memory alone I would be severely limited as to what I could recall and write, but I now find myself reliving every moment with an awful clarity. Yes, I remember so well the increasing torment as I sat in the hatchway, waiting for a wind.

*Lárochka...I think of you all the time and the more I think of you the greater my pain. Lárochka...I have this terrible fear that it was I who killed you. Not directly, of course, but by doing everything wrong. I really thought I could save you, but I should have known better. I can't rid myself of the image of you lying on the ocean bed, with your fur hat and your blonde curls. I can still feel the weight in my hands as I lowered you into the sea. I had no choice but to bury you in that awful way, but now I feel guilty. I'm not sure why. So many doubts and questions. I'm not even sure whether I'll be able to tell anyone what happened. Nobody knows I found you, except for me, and nobody knows I had to bury you, except for me. Lárochka...dear Lárochka...would you mind very much if we kept the whole thing to ourselves? Just something between the two of us? I have this fear that if I tell our story, it will be dissected and distorted in every possible way. I know how these things work. I'm an old man and I don't want to go through all of that. And what good would it do anyway? It won't bring you back. Lárochka…you know that I did the best I could for you. You know that I gave you my bunk and looked after you and held you tightly while you died. That's all that matters to me. This is just between the two of us and maybe it's better to keep it that way. In any case, it may be purely academic, as I'm not at all sure I'm going to be able to get out of the ice. Maybe me joining you on the ocean bed would be the best outcome. Then it really would be our secret, for ever.*

*

Little patches of the lightest wind imaginable crept in from here and there and for the first time in days some high cloud invaded the perfect blue of the sky, moderating the brilliance of the light. The ice floes no longer sparkled, and the sea took on a greyer, more threatening tint.

I was growing tired of waiting for something to happen. I wanted to be moving under sail once more, with at least some feeling of control over my own destiny. Checking our position, I found that we had been pushed all the way back to 10° West, the longitude in which I had found Lárochka. Our latitude was about sixty miles to the north - 79° North – and the anti-clockwise current was now setting us to the south-west. By a strange irony, and after all the efforts to try to get Lárochka to Svalbard, we had ended up in the waters I had been heading for originally. Yes, I was back in the north-west corner of the Greenland Sea, the primary object of the voyage, and I couldn't have cared less. It gave me no pleasure and no sense of achievement. This adventure had already died in my heart. There was nothing about it to celebrate, and there never could be. I just wanted to get back home, should we be lucky enough to clear the ice, as soon as possible.

## 38

I was now, as I said, impatient for something to happen, something which would break the helpless deadlock in which I found myself. This voyage had already gone far beyond the limits of what I thought conceivable but, despite that, nothing could have prepared me for the next part of the story. Something did happen, and even now I shudder at the bitter-sweet memory of it.

Things began quite well. The breeze, such as it was, did in fact settle in very softly from the east. I decided to raise the sail and see if I could navigate out of the ice. It seemed that my best option was to sail as near as I could to a south-south-easterly course, thereby heading directly for warmer water, sailing full and bye on port tack. In a very light wind this was perhaps our best point of sailing, as our windward direction increased the apparent windspeed and kept us ghosting along steadily. Rather than give *M.* over to the self-steering gear, I sat in the hatch and hand-steered, falling off the wind when necessary to by-pass any floes in our path. The density of the floes had increased over the previous days, but there was still plenty of open water for finding a route through the ice without too many deviations.

What a lift it gave me to be moving under sail once more! How reviving it was to hear the gurgle of water under the forefoot! My little yacht had been through so much, and here she was, edging along again as sweetly as ever! I could have felt happy, were it not for the oppressive cloud of Lárochka's death still stifling my spirit and were it not for my constant fear of meeting denser, unnavigable ice. I could not give myself over fully to that most delicious of pleasures – the sensuality of hand-steering a spritely sailboat. I felt better than I had for many days, but my mind was still sluggish and my heart unbearably heavy.

*Lárochka…we're sailing again! Imagine if you had survived, if you had got better. We could have shared spells at the tiller. I could have made you a nice mug of something hot while you steered. I could have shown you how this junk rig works, how easy and clever it is. I need an easy rig here. We're going along OK for the moment. The wind's right and there's enough clear water for us. Being so small helps. She's hardly more than a big dinghy really. I think you would have liked sailing her. I hope you're OK, Lárochka. I think of you all the time. I can't imagine how lonely it must be down there.*

✻

I sailed on, in a kind of daze, wending through the floes, my mind caught in a terrible purgatory between the blinding light and the inescapable darkness; between the crystalline beauty of the sea, ice and sky, and the constant image of Lárochka's body lying on the Arctic seabed.

I sailed on, but after half a day or so at the tiller lines, I began to sense that an escape into open sea was not going to be straightforward. With so much ice around, I could not, of course, give *M.* over to the self-steering gear. This meant that whenever I needed to cook, eat or sleep, I had to lower the sail and once more let *M.* drift along on the current, seriously limiting our progress. Despite the benign conditions, I was suffering more and more from the cold. It was punishing to spend so many hours immobile in the open hatchway and my old joints were aching constantly. My fingers were blue and unresponsive. When trying to sleep I was shivering, despite the heavy coverings. I was not at all sure how long I could maintain this routine.

I struggled on as best I could, for perhaps another day or a day and a half, believing that I soon might reach open water. I had convinced myself that my best chance of escape would be to the south-east, but on the second day of our stop-start progress, I was alarmed to find that the density of the floes was increasing. It was no longer easy to weave a track through them. It required full concentration and a lot of thinking ahead to work out the optimal route. For the first time I was having to manoeuvre dangerously close to the floes. Once or twice, I had to bear right off the wind to avoid a collision. Wherever I looked, whether north, south, east or west, the floes were ever more closely spaced, with fewer and fewer leads of clear water between them. There seemed to be little doubt about it: the sea would soon be unnavigable.

The light wind still held from the east and I was now forced to reduce the sail by a panel or two, to slow *M.* down. This was to give me more time to find a path through the ice and to reduce the impact of a collision. The danger was not so much the bigger floes but those which had almost completely melted and were now no more than heavy fridge-sized lumps floating just at the surface and therefore scarcely visible. One such lump lodged under our transom for a few seconds, thudding dully against *M.*'s hull and threatening to damage her rudder.

I was by now resigned rather than desperate. I would soon have to lower the sail and accept that we were comprehensively entrapped, that there could be no escape from the ice. The likelihood was that *M.*'s hull would sooner or later be crushed by the floes as the pressure built. She would go down and I would go down with her. Maybe I would be able to escape onto a floe, but what good would that do? Either way, I would die of hypothermia. Either way, I would join Lárochka in those cold depths.

*Well, Lárochka, I thought we might be able to find a way out of here, but it seems that once again I was wrong. It's starting to look hopeless. I'll have to stop sailing pretty soon. There's too much ice and it seems to be growing denser and denser. It may sound a strange thing to say, but I envy you now. Whatever you went through, it's over. You're at peace, I suppose. I know now that I'm going to die sometime soon. It may take a day or a week. It may be quick or it may be drawn out. I have no idea. I don't know whether I will be brave or not. I hope I won't scream or blubber. I know that when the moment comes, I will think of you, of your calm face. That will give me strength, Lárochka. And at least I will know that I won't be alone down there. That will be a comfort to me, Lárochka, a great comfort.*

I sat in the hatchway and continued to steer around the encircling floes. I did not want to stop sailing, knowing that once I lowered the sail, it would be for the last time. For seventy years I had been entranced by the motion of a yacht through water, by its ease and sensuality, by its promise of adventure and discovery. I had been immeasurably lucky over the years, but now my luck had run out. And so, I kept on, deferring that final moment for as long as I could and squeezing every last drop out of the life that remained.

# 39

It was weeks since I had seen another vessel and even longer since I had heard any sounds other than those of nature and of *M.* making her way through the water. It took me a while to realise that my ears were picking up a very faint hum coming from somewhere distant. It was scarcely perceptible, the tiniest of vibrations, a delicate undertone to the gentle hiss of water along our leeward side. At first, I thought it was my imagination, but no, the more I listened, the more clearly I could make out a steady mechanical drone. It was a strange sound, somewhat like that of a ship's engine, but smoother, without the distinct throbbing. It was not the sound of an aircraft, and so must be some sort of ship, somewhere well to the east of us.

A ship? Why would a ship be up here? Perhaps it was a cruise ship, maybe one of those Hurtigruten vessels that come to East Greenland occasionally. A fishing boat perhaps? A Norwegian or Icelandic whaler? The ice floes we were amongst would not cause much difficulty for a ship built for the Arctic, and the crews would have real-time access to the ice maps.

And which way was the vessel heading? Would it sail on north or south, somewhere over the horizon, or was it heading west in our direction? That thought caused a rush of unease. It was a reminder that if by some unlikely stroke of luck I escaped the ice and completed the voyage, I would have to face the real world once again, and that I would have to decide whether to tell the story of what happened with Lárochka, or whether to keep it to myself.

I listened carefully and soon convinced myself that the hum was getting louder. It was still faint, all the same, and I had no immediate expectation of seeing anything. I was wrong. Within a minute or two a smudge appeared on the eastern horizon, growing in size at a terrifying rate.

*Bloody hell!*

I had never witnessed anything like it. A huge vessel was heading straight for us at considerable speed, despite the ice, but with no sound apart from that whiny hum. Its superstructure quickly loomed clearly above the ice, and two things struck me about it. The first was its height. It was the equivalent of a ten-storey building rising from deck level. The second was the way the superstructure had been painted. Overall, it was a light blue colour, but the exterior of three of the upper decks had been painted in three colours in horizontal bands: red, above that blue, and above that white. There was no need for this ship to carry an ensign or a national flag. The ship itself was a flag, a Russian flag.

*Jesus!*

The thing was heading straight for us at a good twelve or fifteen knots. A massive Russian ship. What the hell was it doing here? We were well away from the area the Russians consider their own. More importantly, had it seen us or were we about to be erased by the ugly dark blue bow bearing down on us and now less than half a mile away? *M's* white hull and white sail could easily merge into the general scenery. My only hope was that the big rescue-orange circle sewn onto the top panel of her mainsail would draw attention to us. I need not have worried. They knew I was there alright, and they were coming specifically for me.

The whining reduced and the ship slowed. It is hard to describe the effect of seeing something so big and solid and industrial after weeks of contemplating nothing but sky and waves. The ship came to a halt no more than a hundred yards or so to the north, its dark blue hull towering over us. It was clearly a very manoeuvrable vessel. Along the side of hull in massive letters was the word

## РОСАТОМФЛОТ

*Bloody hell!*
*ROSATOMFLOT.* It didn't take a genius to decipher that: Russian Atomic Fleet.
*Jesus!*
It was a Russian nuclear icebreaker. That explained the strange sound of its turbines. I could see the name of the ship painted near the bow:

## Арктика

*Arctic.* I had a vague memory that the Russians had built a small fleet of nuclear icebreakers to help take merchant shipping through the North-East Passage, the iced-up waters to the north of Siberia. Fair enough, but in that case, what the hell was this icebreaker doing a thousand miles to the west, in the Greenland Sea? And why on earth had it stopped? What business had a gargantuan nuclear ship with my tiny cockleshell? Within a split second of asking myself that question, I guessed what the answer might be.

*Jesus! Surely not?*

I took a few deep breaths to calm myself and to get my thoughts in order. Already I could see some activity on the port side of the ship. A black RIB was being lowered from davits into the water. Well, the ship hadn't stopped so that the crew could do a bit of fishing. I knew that they were coming for me, and I was right.

# 40

Oh, the irony of it! The many ironies of this whole cursed voyage! How often had I joked in my books about the Russian girl Olga, always telephoning me when I was near to Bear Island and demanding to be rescued? *You good-breeding Englishman and banking at Coutts. You come rescue me right now!* And what about the imagined visits from the Russian navy when I was mooching about in the Franz Josef Land area? The joke was now on me. Once again, fact was imitating fiction. I had rescued a real Russian girl and now I was about to get a visit from a real Russian ship, and a nuclear-powered one at that. *Yes, sunshine, I told you to keep your bloody mouth shut. You and your stupid imagination!*

I was still ghosting very slowly towards the south-east and I decided that I would ignore the ship and carry on. It wasn't for me to heave-to or change course just because this monstrosity had parked itself a few yards away. Maybe they had other business there, anyway.

This sang-froid was, of course, only skin deep. My relief at the arrival of a vessel that might release me from the trap I found myself in was more than offset by the fear of what may lie behind the ship's appearance. My mind was racing away. What the hell was all this about? Had I been caught on a satellite camera disposing of a Russian girl over the side? And who was this Russian girl? Had a nuclear icebreaker been despatched from its usual station to look for her or whatever vessel she had been on? That seemed inconceivable, but here was a nuclear icebreaker, six hundred feet long and two hundred and fifty feet high, by the looks of it, blotting out the northern horizon and lowering a boat into the water.

*Lárochka…I've got a nasty feeling I'm in big trouble here. Maybe it's as well I never found out who you are or how you came to be in that liferaft. I think I'm going to have a visit very soon from your compatriots and I doubt they are going to be very friendly. Actually, that visit's going to be very soon indeed. They're on their way.*

The RIB was hurtling towards us, skirting round the closely packed ice floes in its way. I tried to compose myself, clearing my head of its accumulated nonsense and reinventing myself, for the moment, as a wide-eyed English innocent. I gave myself an order: *Roger, whatever you do, do not speak Russian! Do not speak Russian or appear to understand any Russian! Play dumb! Play stupid!* Another voice crept in: *No need for you to play stupid, sunshine, just be yourself – that's as stupid as it gets.*

The RIB slowed right down and drew alongside our port quarter. There were about six men and one woman on board, in black uniforms and armed with what looked like Kalashnikovs.

*Jesus!*

These were military-looking types, and this surprised me. As far as I knew, the nuclear icebreakers served a purely commercial role and were nothing to do with the Russian navy. Well, it looked like there was some overlap. Or was this a one-off special mission? *Roger! Don't think! Don't think! Stay innocent! Stay stupid!*

I smiled sweetly at the crew of the accompanying RIB, checked the trim of the mainsail and carried on steering. I looked across to the RIB once more and, in the jolliest voice I could muster, shouted: *lovely day for a sail!* I have no idea whether they heard or understood, over the noise of the RIB's two big outboards, but it made me feel better. I carried on: *perfect wind for getting through the floes, don't you think?* It was by no means easy to put on this air of forced jollity, given all I had been through, but it was the only way I could mask the disquiet that was now gripping me.

The crew member with the most gold on his epaulettes pointed at my mainsail and made arm movements indicating I should lower it. I smiled, looked at the mainsail and carried on sailing. We were in international waters. Nobody had the right to tell me how to manage my own vessel.

The same officer shouted at me. *Hey! Sail! You put down sail!*

I looked at him. *Sorry, old chap, what did you say?*

*Sail! You put down sail! You want I shoot you?* He unslung his Kalashnikov.

I smiled at him again. *Oh, I'm so sorry. I didn't understand.*

I eased off the mainsheet until the sail was billycocking gently and we came to a halt. I was still not inclined to follow orders from anyone, however well-armed they might be. One of the crewmen grabbed hold of a pulpit stanchion to hold the boats together and the outboards were throttled right back to an idle.

Gold epaulettes put his rifle back on his shoulder and leaned over the side of the RIB towards me.

*What you do here?*

*I'm sailing, old chap, and it's a grand day for it, don't you think?*

He turned to his crew, and I heard him mutter something about an *английский дурак – an English idiot*. I reminded myself once more: *Roger – no Russian!* It would be so easy for something to slip out or for me to react to something said in Russian.

I smiled again.

*Anyway, what are you guys up to? That's some ship you've got there – a real beauty! Must be fun crashing through the ice! And thanks for coming over to say hello. That's really kind of you!*

Gold epaulettes stared at me with disbelief. I had no idea whether he had understood what I had said.

*Why you here?*

*Doing an Arctic voyage, old chap. It's been wonderful. Had one bad storm but otherwise pretty damn good. How about you?*

*How long you been here?*

*Been where, old chap? It's quite a while since I left home.*

*How long you been this place, this area?*

*Only a few days. There was no wind for a while.*

*How many people you have on boat?*

*How many people? Just me, old chap. Singlehanded sailor.* I had to stop myself from translating the last phrase into Russian. A lifetime's habit with languages was hard to break.

He turned again to the RIB's crew and gave them the gist of what we had discussed so far, adding something to the effect that *this guy is a total fucking nutcase.*

*I coming on board now.*

*Coming on board? You have no right!* Again, it almost came out automatically. *У вас нет права! You don't have the right!*

He unslung his Kalashnikov again.

*Explain me how you stop me.*

*OK, but why do you want to come on board?*

*I look see you have somebody on boat.*

I let out a jolly laugh.

*Ha! You want to see if there is someone else on board? That's really funny! Look at the size of this boat. Come and have a look in the cabin. It's tiny! There's hardly room for me to sleep, never mind anyone else!*

*You see any other ships here?*

*Other ships? I've not seen anything for weeks.*

*How about things in water? You see any bits of ship? Thing like this –* he tapped the side of the RIB – *thing for save people when ship drown.* I caught myself on the verge of helping him out again with the Russian for liferaft and shipwreck. *Roger! Stay stupid for God's sake!*

I shook my head.

Yes, I shook my head, as I had known I would for some while, and in so doing I formally began the process of erasure that has lasted for so many years. All the doubts I had been having over the previous days crystallised into that one shake of the head. It was now official policy: I had never seen a liferaft, never taken Lárochka on board, never buried her at sea. Perhaps, under other circumstances, I might have been willing to admit to everything that had happened, but the sight of half a dozen Kalashnikovs was the final catalyst for my resolve to stay silent about the whole affair. I had a strong sense that if I admitted anything, or if indeed the Russians found anything, I would be in deep trouble. Whoever Lárochka was, and whatever had happened prior to me finding her, the matter was clearly of considerable importance to the Russians. There was, of course, the possibility that the Russian presence here and the line of their questioning were related to some other matter, but for the moment it seemed wise to assume that this was not the case. The odds on all this having some relationship with Lárochka seemed extremely high.

*You sure you no see anything?*

*Gosh, absolutely! Apart from a bit of bad weather I've been having a great time and not seen anything unusual. What's going on, anyway? Has a ship had a problem or something?*

Gold epaulettes studied me closely.

*No. No problem. I come look on your boat now.*

He spoke a few words to his crew, who unslung their rifles and held them at the ready. I got the message.

*Well, please do come on board. It's a great pleasure to see you.*

Gold epaulettes crossed nimbly from the RIB, over *M.'s* lifeline and dropped down into the cockpit, almost putting his foot into the toilet bucket as he went.

I held out my hand.

*Welcome aboard. My name's Roger. It's ever so good of you to come to say hello.*

He shook my hand briefly.

*OK. I look down now.*

I dropped back down into the cabin and sat on my bunk. Gold epaulettes leaned forward and looked down the hatch from where he was standing in the cockpit.

*You see. No room to swing a cat, as we say.*

*Cat? You have cat with you?*

*Ha! No, no. There's only me.*

Gold epaulettes knelt on the bridge deck and pushed his shoulders through the hatch, so that he could see the whole cabin, fore and aft.

*Is small. You have one bed?*

*Yes! Just enough room for me.*

I could see him studying everything in sight, slowly and carefully.

A terrible thought hit me. *The ship's log! What if he asks to see the ship's log?* There were very few entries since I had found Lárochka, but they were there nonetheless, giving the rough time I had found the liferaft, when I had set sail with Larochka aboard and so on. There were explicit references to a 'Russian liferaft' and a 'Russian girl'. What was worse, I had, as was my habit, made a quick sketch of the liferaft. *Jesus!* Usually both my logbooks, the ship's and my personal log, sit on top of whichever paper chart I am using, on the chart table. They would have been obvious for somebody looking for evidence. Luckily, they were under the chart, not drawing attention to themselves.

Gold epaulettes let his shoulders drop further through the hatch so that he was looking directly aft through the gap between the companionway steps.

*What you have there?*

*Oh, just stores and things. Bags of clothes. Spare rope. That kind of thing.*

*You move things so I can see.*

*No problem whatsoever.*

I started on the starboard side, pulling out bags and containers. As I worked, I had another awful thought.

*Lárochka's oilskins!*

I had stuffed them into a bag on the port side and had forgotten about them.

*Jesus!*

What if he looks in the bag and recognises them somehow, or sees that they are far too small for me? It was becoming obvious that a proper search of *M.* would very quickly reveal that Lárochka had been on board. I crossed over to the port quarter berth, hoping I would find a way to keep the bag out of sight without gold epaulettes getting suspicious.

It wasn't necessary. I heard some Russian coming from the RIB's radio, evidently from the ship. Gold epaulettes withdrew his head from the hatch and had a brief exchange with his crew.

*Никто. Ничего. Nobody. Nothing.*

He gave some more orders and I felt the rocking of the boat as he crossed back to the RIB.

I stuck my head through the hatch to see what was going on. Gold epaulettes was talking to the ship on the RIB's radio. I couldn't catch the gist of what was being said. The crewman let go of the pushpit stanchion and the RIB eased forward. I thought that was it and was about to say goodbye. The RIB moved as far as our bow and one of the crew started to attach a line to the big mooring cleat on the foredeck.

*Bloody hell! They're not taking me in tow, for God's sake!*

*Hey! What the hell are you doing!*

Gold epaulettes laughed.

*You no worry! You coming with us! You be OK!*

I heard a whine as the ship's turbines started up. *Jesus!* The ship! It started to move forward, turning hard to port as it went. *What the hell's going on?* The ship came right round us, far too close for my comfort, its slab sides towering over *M.*'s tiny hull. Once it was ahead of us, it straightened its course. I was amazed at its beam – well over a hundred feet. The RIB set off after it, with *M.* in tow.

I grabbed the tiller lines to keep our course steady as we raced along. The ship was obviously going slowly, for our sake, but we were still making eight or ten knots. I yelled again.

*Hey! What the hell are you doing?*

Gold epaulettes looked back and grinned, giving a big thumbs up.

*Jesus Christ! What the hell's going on?*

An hour earlier I had been forcing a slow passage through the floes. Now here I was, dragged along by an overpowered RIB, chockful of Kalashnikov-wielding Russians, and just a few yards aft of the monstrously wide stern of a nuclear icebreaker.

*What the hell are they doing?*

I checked the compass. We were heading east-south-east. For how long? How long would my cleat or foredeck hold, given the strain they were under? Where was I being taken? To another Russian ship? A proper navy ship? Why had they not just taken me and left *M.* behind? Or did they want to examine her more thoroughly?

*Jesus!*

I let go of the tiller for a moment and ducked below to grab the logbooks off the chart table. I would have thrown them over the side there and then, but a couple of the RIB's crewmen were keeping a permanent eye on their tow. There was no way I could do it without being seen. I put the logbooks on the shelf under the bridge deck, where I could get at them quickly if an opportunity arose to drop them over the side unnoticed.

The ice around us grew even thicker and before long the sea was hidden under a layer of tightly packed floes, devoid of any clear water. I stared at the solid expanse of white. We were heading roughly in the direction I had been sailing and it was clear that I would not have got very far.

*Bloody hell!*

I had been in a much worse position than I realised. For the icebreaker these melting summer floes were no more than an annoyance: I read later that the ship could make progress through solid pack-ice ice nine feet thick. It carried on at the same speed, creating a clear channel thirty yards wide.

We were dragged along for at least half an hour. I had no idea where we were going or what lay in wait at the end. I was caught up in something way beyond my understanding.

The ice floes began to thin out again, creating more and more open water. *They're taking me to another ship, for sure. Jesus! What a mess!* I remembered the well-worn maxim: *no good deed goes unpunished.*

Another few minutes and we were in open sea. I would have rejoiced at the sight were I not convinced that we were being delivered somewhere for a proper search and interrogation. The ship began to turn to starboard, but the RIB did not follow it. It slowly throttled back, allowing our momentum to carry us along while one of the crew took up the slack in the towrope. When the RIB was beside the bow, he un-cleated the line and the RIB manoeuvred around until it was once again alongside our port beam.

Gold epaulettes pointed ahead with a wide sweep of the arm.

*Ice is gone! Russians good people! We take you out of ice! You go home, Englishman! Bye-bye!*

# 41

The reversal of fortune was so rapid and so unexpected that for a minute or two I was unable to move. It was all too much to process. I didn't even wave to gold epaulettes as he sped off back to the icebreaker. We were out of the ice. In a few minutes the Russians would be gone. Nobody was going to ransack the boat. Nobody was going to interrogate me. We were free. We had a fair wind. I hooked up the self-steering gear and trimmed the mainsail to balance us on a course roughly east of south. I wasn't concerned about an accurate heading. Anywhere south would do.

By now the RIB was back aboard the icebreaker. The ship headed north-west, back towards the ice. I sat in the hatchway, still dumbfounded by the turn of events, and at the same time light-headed from the relief of the survivor. Within a few minutes the ship was gone, save for the whine of its turbines.

I knew what I had to do. I took the logbooks from the shelf under the bridge deck and ripped them to shreds, page by page, at the same time throwing each handful of paper over the lee side. For a sailor, this was a kind of sacrilege, but it had to be done and with each handful that floated away I felt better. As each physical trace of what had happened disappeared, my spirit lifted. I was liberating myself from the need to tell, from the duty to explain. At the same time, I was binding myself more closely to Lárochka.

When the logbooks were gone, I went below and pulled out Lárochka's waterproofs from the bag on the port quarter berth. I wrapped them in a plastic bag, along with a small grapple anchor I used for the inflatable dinghy I had on board and dropped the bag overboard. To complete the job of erasing all traces of the voyage so far, I sat on my bunk with my cameras and camcorder and deleted every photo and video clip I had taken. I could not destroy my Greenland to Svalbard chart, as I still needed it, but I carefully rubbed out all my pencilled-in noon positions and dates. There were tracks from previous voyages still on the chart and I left them intact.

The whole exercise was so therapeutic and so liberating that I began to wonder whether all the memories that we create and carry with us are no more than an unnecessary burden. Why do we bind ourselves so tightly to a past that is gone and therefore has no substance? It occurred to me that a man who lives only in the present can never age. There are, of course, some memories which are so strong that they merge into the present and become part of it. That is my experience with Lárochka. She is a living presence and always will be.

*Lárochka...I'm sailing home. The wind is still in the east, a perfect breeze for getting us south. We are out of the ice, but only thanks to your compatriots. I thought I would be able to sail out, but I was wrong. We were trapped by much thicker floes to the south. The icebreaker must have known this. Lárochka…I still find it hard to believe: a Russian nuclear icebreaker diverted for an hour or two to create a passage out of the ice for us. Lárochka…I'm not sure what to say. They were good to us, but there was no doubt they were looking for somebody or something. Was it you? Was it some trace of the vessel you were on? Maybe. Maybe not. I don't think I will ever know. Anyway, they asked whether I had seen anybody, whether I had seen a liferaft. I said no, Lárochka. No. I had not seen anything. I denied your existence. In many ways I feel bad about that. I could have said yes. I could have said that I found a girl called Lárochka adrift on the ocean. I could have said that I cared for her as best I could, that she died in my arms, that I buried her at sea with as much ceremony and dignity as I could muster. I could have said that even though we never exchanged a single word she had become a dear friend to me. I could have said all that, but I denied everything. Was it the right thing to do, Lárochka, or was it cowardly of me? I don't know the answer to that. I have no idea what this business is all about, and to be frank, I really don't care. I had no wish to be interrogated, no desire to explain our story, no desire for the whole thing to be picked over by hungry, uncomprehending vultures. As I said to you a while ago, this is just between you and me, and that's how I want to keep it. If you think I'm wrong, then I'm truly sorry and I ask you to forgive me. I'm an old man, Lárochka. Even though from here on I will try to live only in the present moment, I know well enough that that present moment cannot last for much longer. I still wish that we could have changed places, Lárochka, but the least I can do is to carry you with me until I too am at rest.*

# 42

I have little memory of the voyage back to Scotland. I navigated but wrote nothing down. I watched the sea, as usual, but my mind was elsewhere. I saw the occasional ship and fishing boat as we approached and crossed the Arctic Circle, but my interest went no further than establishing that we were not on a collision course. There were the inevitable little gales as we ran the gauntlet of the jet stream but, compared to the storm I had endured with Lárochka in my arms, they were lightweight trifles. I was there, aboard *M.*, but the usual close connection with my yacht had been severed. I was going through all the motions, honed to precision over many years, but my heart was not in it.

I was tired, too. Usually, by that stage of a voyage I am so acclimatised to life at sea and so attuned to the twenty-four hour round of sleep, watch and eat, that my energy levels are at their peak. This time, I was listless and would happily have slept for hours on end. Only habit and an inbuilt discipline stopped me from surrendering to the temptation to escape my thoughts through sleep. Those thoughts were simple and repetitive. I could not rid myself of the image of Lárochka's fur hat descending under the surface of the sea. I could feel the weight of her body and still sense in my nerves and muscles the impulse to pull her back up again. Along with that, I had established in my mind a picture of her lying on the seabed, mouth slightly open, her face still framed by her blond curls, and I could not rid myself of it. Whenever I thought of her, those were the twin images I saw: her fur hat lowered into the ocean; her body lying on the dark seabed. I knew that I was being consumed by guilt, but I could not rationalise why. Is one's best never enough? Was my inability to save her a result of my carelessness as regards my own well-being? Ought I to have enrolled on first-aid courses and survival courses and taught myself much more than I knew about hypothermia and how to treat it? Should one spend one's life preparing for things that may never happen, or should one just get on with it regardless? I could find no answers to the questions that tormented me. They spun round in my head, day after day, never getting closer to any kind of resolution.

The decision to obliterate all records of the voyage seemed increasingly sensible. My own self-interrogation of what had happened was bad enough. How would it be if every man and his dog were having their say on the matter? The thought was unbearable. How could anyone who had not been there have even the slightest notion of what I, or indeed Lárochka, had gone through? And how could I ever explain or communicate every subtlety and nuance of what happened? I knew that this was impossible and that it was therefore better that I keep quiet.

We reached the east coast of Shetland and with the wind in the west, made rapid progress south into the Moray Firth. I made my usual close pass of the Captain oil field and early on a summer's morning in late August picked up the low smudge of the Moray hills. By late afternoon we were in range, and I called up the harbourmaster on my handheld VHF radio.

*You'll be off the harbour by six-thirty? Nae bother. I'll be out to tow you in.*

The harbourmaster was, as ever, true to his word. He came alongside a few hundred yards off the harbour wall, and I passed him the line I had prepared. In we went, at half tide, up the narrow entrance passage before a turn hard to port into the outer basin. Somebody up on the quayside waved and I waved back. We crossed into the inner basin and the harbourmaster put me alongside my berth, letting go my line. I hopped onto the pontoon to secure a couple of temporary warps. The harbourmaster circled round in the basin, came alongside. and handed me an envelope.

*A letter for you.*

*Who from?*

*I dinnae ken who he was. Nae seen him before. An old guy. Came into the office for just a wee minute. Maybe a week or two after you were away. Said to give this to you if y'ever came back. An' if you didnae come back, to put it in the trash.*

I took the envelope.

*Thanks.*

The harbourmaster moved away to moor his runabout on the other side of the basin.

I went below and studied the outside of the envelope. It had my name written on it in large, slightly shaky capitals. I slit the envelope open with my rigging knife and took out the folded sheet from inside.

I recognised the style of writing. It was that of a man taught copperplate in a strict classroom, but of a man who wrote rarely and had no ease with the process. Age too had robbed the letters of their smooth curvature. It was a strained and shaky hand. I read the short letter:

> *Dear Roger*
> *If you are reading this letter then it means you got back OK. I hope your voyage was good. I came to see you that time because I was afraid for you. Don't ask me why. Anyway, we sailors have to stick together.*
> *Yours ever*
> *Joshua Arnott*
> *PS I saw your boat Roc one time when I was coming into the Gladstone River. She was moored fore and aft on the piles there. I was going to come and say hello but by then you had already left.*

I was stunned. The Gladstone River! I thought back and did a quick calculation. I was there in 1974, when cruising the Queensland coast after sailing in the Singlehanded TransTasman Race. I remembered the river and how tricky it was to get lines to those mooring piles in an engineless yacht. I was in my mid-twenties at the time. Joshua Arnott? The name meant nothing to me. Nearly fifty years had passed since he had seen my yacht *Roc,* just the once. Unable to make any sense of it, I put the letter back in its envelope and slid the envelope into the pocket of my fleece.

*

*Lárochka…I'm home. There were so many times when I thought I would never make it back, but here I am. I'm lying on my bunk in harbour, enjoying the evening quiet, thinking about the voyage, thinking about you. The voyage itself means nothing. By a series of unplanned circumstances, I ended up almost exactly where I was heading and so in one sense I achieved my goal. I could not imagine a more hollow success. It happened despite me and as I said, it's meaningless. What pains me now is how far away you are. Well over a thousand sea miles. I can't bear the thought of you all alone up there, so far away, so alone. And in winter you'll be iced in, too. I will think of you during the long winter nights. That I promise, Lárochka. I'm not sure why I care so much. Maybe I should just forget you, push you right out of my mind and pretend you never existed. The thought is tempting but I know it's impossible. You will always be there in the forefront of my thoughts. Maybe one day I will find the courage to write about you. Maybe the time will come when I feel able to tell our story; maybe it won't. Somehow, I doubt it, but if it that time does come, I promise I will do the best I can for you. Think about it…people you don't know, complete strangers in another country, will read your name over and over. Lárochka. Lárochka. They will picture your fur hat and your blonde curls. They will think about you lying on that distant seabed. You won't be quite so alone. You will take on another existence. You will live again, Lárochka. If the time does come when I am able to tell our story, I will try to give you back the life I could not save.*

# POSTSCRIPT

I went through all the post-voyage rituals as quickly as I could, dismantling the rig, craning out the mast and hull, preparing for the road journey and so on, in just a couple of days. I avoided people in the harbour as much as I could and was non-committal when asked how the voyage had gone.

*Fine, thanks. Fine.*

Once home, I made no attempt to find out whether there had been any reports of a missing Russian yachtswoman or whether a Russian vessel of some sort had been lost in the High Arctic. I have plenty of sailing friends in Russia and could no doubt have found out more about Lárochka and her background. Something held me back. I had shared the moment of her death in the most extreme and intimate of ways and I wanted to leave that moment just as it was, without qualification and without external dissection. Even though I am not at all sure that she knew where she was, or that she was aware that she was being cared for and cradled into death by an aging Englishman, I like to think that she was in some way present until the final hours.

It was a shared secret, and it has taken some years, along with the various insanities of pandemic and war, to bring me to the point where I am ready to reveal it. This story has been locked inside me for too long and I must purge myself of its weight. Should there be any repercussions, I will try to bear them with equanimity.

As for Joshua Arnott, I did make enquiries. Some years ago, quite by chance, I had reestablished contact with a friend I had made when cruising the Queensland coast in the mid-1970's, Ian Kirk. He and his then wife Sally had been at Gladstone when I was there, cruising in their yacht *Wyuna*. They had got to know Joshua, and Ian and Joshua had maintained their friendship for many years afterwards. Ian sent me a few photographs of Joshua taken at the time. They showed a lean, white-bearded man already well into his sixties. Ian also sent me a photograph of a page from *Wyuna's* visitors' book, showing the facetious comment I had written. The date of the entry was the sixth of July 1974. The next entry, just captured by the same photograph, and dated the twelfth of July 1974, was by Joshua Arnott. I recognised the same copperplate, albeit a little more regular, as in his letter, and the same signature with its ornate A to begin the Arnott. It seems that Joshua and his beautiful wooden cutter *Sirius* were well-known up and down that coastline. Age and failing health had finally confined him to the Port of Airlie marina on the central Queensland coast, after which friends in the sailing community had arranged for him to go into sheltered accommodation in the nearby town of Cannonvale. Joshua had died there in his early nineties, many years ago.

In conclusion, I offer a final confession. I began this story by describing it as an old man's tale. Although I have tried to tell that tale as accurately as my memory allows, a note of caution is in order. It may be that I have misremembered; that my aging brain has played tricks on me. It may even be that despite its vivid and unwavering hold on my mind, the narrative is no more than a construct of my imagination. I can no longer be sure, but whether it is or not is of little importance, as every story creates its own reality and harbours its own truths.

.